D0049360

Praise for
The Spirituality That Heals

"Michael Youssef leads us out of the shadowlands of superficial spirituality into the promise land of genuine sanctifying spirituality. Prepare to be challenged and changed!"

>—HANK HANEGRAAFF, host of the *Bible Answer Man* radio program
>and author of *The Prayer of Jesus*

"In a broken, hurting world that longs for hope, Michael Youssef has provided a remedy for our souls that is both biblical and practical. Read this and embrace the healing power of God."

>—DR. JOSEPH M. STOWELL, president of Moody Bible Institute

"Michael Youssef is one of the most gifted pastors of our generation. I recommend *The Spirituality That Heals* to all who seek the healing power of Jesus Christ."

>—LARRY BURKETT, author of *Nothing to Fear: The Key to Cancer Survival*
>and chairman of the board of Crown Financial Ministries

"Michael Youssef does an inspiring job of teaching the remarkable truth about the work of the Holy Spirit. His book will invite you to empty yourself and seek to be filled with God's Spirit."

>—NICKY CRUZ, international evangelist
>and author of *One Holy Fire* and *Run, Baby, Run*

THE
Spirituality
That
HEALS

THE
Spirituality
That
HEALS

GOD'S PROVISION
FOR YOUR SOUL'S
DEEPEST NEED

MICHAEL YOUSSEF

WATERBROOK
PRESS

THE SPIRITUALITY THAT HEALS
PUBLISHED BY WATERBROOK PRESS
2375 Telstar Drive, Suite 160
Colorado Springs, Colorado 80920
A division of Random House, Inc.

All Scripture quotations, unless otherwise indicated, are taken from the *Holy Bible, New International Version®*. NIV®. Copyright © 1973, 1978, 1984 by International Bible Society. Used by permission of Zondervan Publishing House. All rights reserved. Scripture quotations marked (KJV) are taken from the *King James Version.*

ISBN 1-57856-555-3

Library of Congress Cataloging-in-Publication Data
Youssef, Michael.
   The spirituality that heals : God's provision for your soul's deepest need / Michael Youssef.—1st ed.
     p. cm.
   Includes bibliographical references.
   ISBN 1-57856-555-3
   1. Spirituality. 2. Healing—Religious aspects—Christianity. I. Title.
BV4509.5.Y68 2003
234' .131—dc21   2002013844

Printed in the United States of America
2003—First Edition

10 9 8 7 6 5 4 3 2 1

CONTENTS

The fruit of the Spirit is love, joy, peace, patience,
kindness, goodness, faithfulness, gentleness and self-control.
Against such things there is no law.

—GALATIANS 5:22-23

One

In Search of a Genuine Spirituality

Only the Holy Spirit Can Heal Our Deepest Needs

Healing!

Mention the word, and anyone who needs healing or knows of someone who needs healing immediately pays attention.

These days healers abound. From the faith healers of the Philippines to the herbal medicine men of China to the chanters of Hinduism to the positive mental attitude disciples to the charismatic Christian healers, all who promise healing touch an exposed nerve in our psyche. Intuitively, we recognize that we need to be restored. We sense that we are not whole, either physically or emotionally or spiritually. And we instinctively seek to be made whole.

Given the very basic nature of our need for wholeness, it is not surprising that healing and spirituality have become the Siamese twins of our modern world. Even with all of our sophisticated medical technology, the need for healing and wholeness has driven many to a quest for spirituality.

In the past two decades, thousands of new books have addressed the subject of spirituality. And over the past ten years, the most popular television talk shows have returned again and again to the topic of spirituality.

This intense interest is evidence of a deep and genuine human desire to become something that many in our society realize they are not. They want to connect with their spiritual nature.

At the root of this quest is a deep-seated sense of restlessness—an unavoidable feeling of being unsettled. We have finally come to realize that technology alone cannot solve all our problems, especially the illnesses and diseases of the body and the mind. Time after time, men and women suffering from a life-threatening condition are told by the best minds in the medical field: "We've done all that medical science can do. I'm sorry, but we can't do anything to help you." Deep inside, we wonder if there is something in the unseen spirit world that can bring us to greater wholeness.

A University of Chicago poll revealed that 67 percent of Americans believe in the supernatural. Forty-two percent said they have had contact with the dead.[1] Another source claimed that sixty million Americans, in one way or another, are involved in the New Age movement.[2]

But that only begins to tell the story. One out of four Americans say they believe in reincarnation.[3] Forty million Americans depend on astrology, with a billion or more people worldwide looking to the stars for guidance.[4] In addition, more than one hundred thousand Americans are registered as witches or warlocks.[5] So widespread is the interest in all forms of spirituality that *Forbes* magazine estimated the New Age movement had created a 3.5 billion dollar market![6]

This quest for spirituality is thriving even in America's heartland. Krishna College in Iowa claims that its Hindu meditation practices brought about the fall of the Iron Curtain in Eastern Europe. Maharishi Mahesh Yogi, father of transcendental meditation, has declared mountainous Watauga County, North Carolina, to be the spiritual center of the universe. He is building a seven-thousand-acre residential and religious training center there called Heavenly Mountain, where meditation will be the guiding force for peace and harmony.

SHADOW SPIRITUALITY VERSUS TRUE SPIRITUALITY

The New Age movement, perhaps more than any other entity, does the most to combine the human desire for healing with a form of spirituality. Building on the endorsement of many of Hollywood's best-known celebrities, the New Age movement has made spirituality something that is not only acceptable, but highly desirable.

But this is spirituality only in the loosest sense. In truth it is "shadow spirituality"—merely a shadow of the real thing. Don't allow these false teachers to mislead you. We need to lay hold of the only true spirituality there is—the only form of spiritual power that genuinely heals. We need the discernment to recognize the differences between shadow spirituality and the true spirituality of God. It is only in God's true spirituality that we find solace for our heart's deepest longings—healing for our soul, peace for our mind, and comfort for our emotions. That healing, peace, and comfort come only when we are committed to the pursuit of true spirituality.

THE "SELF" MOVEMENT

Look around you and you'll be amazed at all the manifestations of the "self" movement—one of the clearest evidences of the modern-day obsession with spirituality. Many of our schools emphasize self-esteem in our children above some of the basic skills and knowledge they will need to function successfully as adults. We hear frequent discussions about self-actualization, self-empowerment, and self-improvement. It is as if all the answers to our problems are to be found by looking within.

Worshiping the one true and living God—which is the only effective medicine that brings healing and wholeness—is replaced by self-worship, self-gratification, and self-glorification. The shadow spirituality of New Age philosophy puts God down and elevates self. In sharp contrast, true spirituality elevates God far above all else, including the self.

Shadow spirituality calls upon individuals to look inward, to put themselves at the center of the universe. True spirituality calls upon an individual to look outward and upward, to put God at the center of all life, and to grow in understanding and in relationship with Him.

Shadow spirituality teaches the "god within." This god is not the Triune God revealed in the Bible, but rather a force that supposedly compels a person to "improve himself." This god is nothing more than man's ability to learn, grow, and develop—all of which are God's gifts to us. None of these abilities, however, is capable of regenerating the human heart.

True spirituality that heals is rooted in the fact that God is transcendent. He stands outside and apart from His creation. He is the omnipotent, omniscient, omnipresent One who loves unconditionally and who desires fellowship with all mankind. But He relates to us on His terms, not on ours. God is holy—He stands separate from humanity. He is utterly righteous, just, and sovereign over all that He has created.

True spirituality, therefore, is dependent on God's Spirit coming into a person's life. God indwells a person as that person responds in faith to Jesus Christ as Savior and Lord. This is the exact opposite of New Age shadow spirituality, which contends that the "god within" merely needs to be awakened and coaxed into actualizing activities. Someone once asked,

"How can a person find the god within when that same person is the one who is confused about what he's looking for?" It's a valid question!

A Failure to Acknowledge Sin

When all the feel-good emotions and Hollywood glitz are stripped from the shadow spirituality of New Age teaching, one quickly realizes the New Age is not all that new. It is actually the oldest of all philosophies, dating back to the Garden of Eden, where the first man and woman thought they could be like God. Indeed, they sought to *be* God.

New Age teachers falsely declare that since the unconscious is really God all along, it is possible for us to become God. Further, the New Age system teaches that God is everywhere, at the core of everything and everyone. Ironically, this belief is held to be true regardless of whether a person accepts the existence of God.

The message of true spirituality teaches just the opposite. All humanity is born with a missing dimension caused by the sin of mankind's wanting to live independently of God. True spirituality reveals the *only* way to fill that void through repentance of sin, faith in Jesus Christ, and the indwelling power of God's Spirit. This is the spirituality that makes us whole. It is only when God's Spirit opens our blind spiritual eyes that we truly begin to understand ourselves and recognize our own darkness, propensity for evil, and moral corruption—in other words, our sinfulness. True spirituality calls us to recognize that our desperate inner need is not a need for independence, but rather a consuming need for a Savior.

The New Age teaches that there is no sin and therefore no need for salvation. Healing and wholeness are possible if a person simply learns to focus the energy that exists in his own soul. True spirituality teaches that sin is the state of all mankind and that all are in need of a Savior. Healing and wholeness are possible only as the person yields the totality of his life to Christ Jesus and allows the Holy Spirit to renew his mind, mend his brokenness, strengthen his weaknesses, and deliver his soul from evil.

Is All Spirituality Good?

The ascendance of shadow spirituality has influenced even traditional churches. Many members of mainline churches have bought into various aspects of shadow spirituality, and two great heresies have resulted. One is the heresy that all spirituality is good spirituality. The second is the heresy that all religions are good as long as they promote peace and unity. Millions are deceived on these points.

In the following chapters, I will point the way to true spirituality. As we examine the differences between true spirituality and shadow spirituality, we will confront the falsehood that "the more a person becomes spiritually minded, the closer that person is drawn to God." The world is not divided into the spiritual and the unspiritual, but rather, all of human life has a spiritual dimension, and our choice is between good and evil, not spiritual and nonspiritual.

The second goal of this book is to confront the misconception that all spirituality that promotes peace and unity is good. There is no lasting peace apart from knowing Christ Jesus as one's Savior. There can be no genuine unity apart from a mutual declaration that Jesus is Lord of all. Hence, there is only *one* spiritual path that leads to true peace and unity.

SPIRITUALITY AND WHOLENESS

Our longing for wholeness can motivate us to seek the true spirituality that is rooted in the Bible and in relationship with the Holy Spirit. In His Word, God gives us a clear standard for what it means to be spiritual and to pursue the spirituality that brings genuine healing. The more we understand God's plan for developing biblical spirituality, the more we will experience His healing.

New Age teaching aims for two ultimate goals: enlightenment and empowerment. It is aimed at helping a person reach an improved state of emotional health, which includes a strong self-esteem and balance of spirit, mind, and body. Biblical truth enables us to achieve a similar, but not identical, goal. The goals of biblical spirituality are that mankind might know the light of the world, Jesus Christ, and that we might experience wholeness of body, mind, and spirit in becoming like God's Son, Jesus Christ. True spirituality acknowledges that this healing can only come as the Holy Spirit of God is invited to do a work of transformation and wholeness within our lives.

In New Age philosophy, a person knows she is whole when she feels happy and lives in harmony with all mankind—in other words, when she declares herself to be whole. In true spirituality, a person is made whole when she reflects the character-likeness of Jesus Christ. A person is whole when God says she is whole in the likeness of Christ.

True biblical spirituality does the work of healing us and making us whole, fulfilling the deepest longing of our souls. Let's begin the journey that will show us how the Holy Spirit does His healing work in our lives.

Two

The Holy Spirit's Healing Work

What the Bible Teaches About God's Activity in Our Lives

Many of today's teachers of spirituality declare that the "god within" is the essence of spirituality. This lie has even invaded many churches. I once had a two-hour debate with a minister of a mainline Protestant church who not only believes spirituality is whatever you want it to be but teaches this belief to his congregation. And sadly, those who hold to the position that spirituality is defined exclusively by the Bible are often accused of being intolerant.

I am willing to be considered intolerant as long as what I declare is the truth of God's Word: that the *only* source of true spirituality is the third Person of the Trinity, the Holy Spirit.

THE PERSON AND WORK OF THE HOLY SPIRIT

The Bible tells us the Holy Spirit is a Person (see John 14:26; 16:13-15). He is the third member of the Trinity. The Holy Spirit is not an impersonal force, so He must never be referred to as "it." The Holy Spirit is more aptly and fully referred to as "The Holy Spirit of Almighty God."

The Holy Spirit works in us personally. He witnesses, convicts, glorifies

Christ, leads and guides, teaches and commands, intercedes, and helps. The Holy Spirit desires God's best for us. He prays through us that God's perfect will might be done in our lives. The Holy Spirit can be lied to, quenched, and grieved. These are all qualities that reflect the essence of personhood.

One of the foremost word pictures of the Holy Spirit found in Scripture is the title *Breath of God.* In fact, the first word picture associated with the Spirit is that of breath—of something that makes the air move, even to the point of vigorous or violent motion. It's a picture of energy released, an outward-moving force of power. The Hebrew word for spirit is *ruach,* which means "breath" or "wind."

God created the earth out of nothing other than His spoken word—expelled by His breath into the shapeless, meaningless void. God shaped some dust of the earth, breathed life into it, and created man. Throughout history, the Holy Spirit has been the Creator of man's inner, spiritual nature. He is the Creator of true community, human gifts and talents, and our spiritual nature.

When we read the Old Testament, we see that God's Spirit is credited with:

- controlling the course of history (see Isaiah 34:16).
- revealing God's truth and will (see Nehemiah 9:30 and Zechariah 7:12).
- teaching God's people the way of faithfulness (see Psalm 143:10 and Isaiah 48:16).
- equipping individuals for leadership (see Genesis 31; Numbers 11; and Deuteronomy 34).

It is the Holy Spirit of God who instigated the conception of Jesus in the virgin's womb and who completely filled Jesus from the moment of His conception. The Spirit of God is portrayed as being ever active, creative, sovereignly controlling, revealing, and enabling. He is the outward manifestation of God to all believers today.

In John 14–16, Jesus made it clear that after His resurrection, the Holy Spirit would be His personal representative on earth. This truth is crucial: No other person is Jesus' representative on earth—no pope or bishop, no minister, priest, teacher, or televangelist. The Holy Spirit alone is Jesus' representative.

The Holy Spirit leads us to God in numerous ways. He convicts us of sin, opening our blind spiritual eyes and enabling us to believe in Jesus. The Holy Spirit interprets the Scripture and illuminates the human heart to understand the Word of God. He does whatever is necessary to create, sustain, and deepen our relationship with God the Father through Jesus the Son.

As we consider the work and person of the Holy Spirit, let's examine four of the most basic teachings.

1. The Holy Spirit Renews Us

As the Holy Spirit does His work as a member of the Trinity, He renews us and transforms us into the image of Christ. His work of renewing and transforming is done in relation to God the Father and God the Son.

Christ Jesus was God's only begotten Son dwelling among mankind in physical form. When Jesus ascended and returned to the Father, the Holy Spirit fulfilled Jesus' promise (see especially John 14:15-20,26-27; 15:26; 16:5-16). The Spirit is God dwelling among mankind today in an unlimited form.

Christ Jesus was the full expression of God the Father—Jesus said that if you saw Him, you saw the Father (see John 14:6-7,9-11). There was nothing of God that was not present in Jesus and nothing in Jesus that was not entirely God. He was the embodiment of God's character, personality, love, plan, and purpose. The Spirit who empowered and motivated and filled Christ Jesus was the same Spirit who created everything we know as life on this planet. The only difference between God the Father and God the Son was that the Son willingly chose to temporarily limit Himself to time and space and to a physical human body.

The Holy Spirit is the full expression of God the Father and God the Son. Jesus said He would send the Spirit to enable us to become more like Him (see John 14:10-14,19-20,26; 15:4-17; 16:8,13-15). There is nothing of the character of God the Father or God the Son that is not evident in the Holy Spirit. He is the fullness of God's character, love, presence, plan, and purpose. The only difference between God the Holy Spirit and God the Son is that the Holy Spirit chooses to work individually with each one of us, drawing us to God, and once we come to a point of belief, dwelling within all those who accept Jesus as their Savior.

The Holy Spirit Is Involved in Our Salvation

As God draws us to Himself, the Holy Spirit is fully involved—from our initial hunger for truth to our acceptance of Jesus as God's Son and our Savior. The Holy Spirit begins His work by convicting us that we are without God and revealing that the penalty for dying without God is eternal separation from God in a place the Bible calls hell. The Holy Spirit further convicts us of the sin that separates us from God. This is the sin that we all are born into—the sin common to all mankind. The Holy Spirit reveals the truth that Jesus Christ was sent to die on a cross as an atoning sacrifice in place of sinful humanity, so that whoever believes in Jesus as Savior will receive forgiveness of sin and the gift of eternal life (see John 3:16). The Holy Spirit reveals that we are sinners who can't save ourselves. Around us, the Holy Spirit sets into place circumstances, relationships, and situations that help move us ever closer to Jesus Christ so that we might see and accept Him as Savior and then seek to follow Him as our Lord.

Rabbi Slostowski, a professor of Talmud in the rabbinical seminary in Tel Aviv, once hated the Lord Jesus Christ. His resentment was so great that he verbally attacked a young Jewish convert for reading the New Testament. The young man replied by giving the rabbi a copy of the Hebrew New Testament. That night, Rabbi Slostowski stayed up until three in the morning reading about the Nazarene who claimed to be the Messiah. The Holy Spirit moved upon his heart, and the rabbi confessed that Jesus, indeed, is Savior and Lord. He later wrote that he had found more than two hundred passages in the New Testament that proved beyond a shadow of doubt that Jesus is Messiah.

The Holy Spirit put a certain student in this rabbi's path and compelled that student to give his professor a copy of the Hebrew New Testament. As the professor read Jesus' life-giving words, the Holy Spirit moved upon his heart. The Spirit convicted him of his need to confess that Jesus is Savior.

Sadly, two teachings common in New Age philosophy directly contradict this work of the Holy Spirit. First, those within the New Age movement—and even in some churches—would have us believe that if we truly understand ourselves, we will realize that we are one with the soul of the universe and that each of us is god. This teaching, a recycling of ancient pagan belief, asserts that we all have the nature of god at our human core. The New Age movement claims that if we will simply peel away the layers of negative thinking, bad feelings, and hurtful memories, we will become self-empowered and self-actualized, all in the name of the "god" that lies latent in the nature of our souls.

If a person is caught up in defining himself as his own god, he certainly doesn't want the Holy Spirit to convict him of sin or help him become Christlike. The goal of shadow spirituality is not to become like Christ Jesus, but rather to become "more of who you are"—to get to the pure essence of *self*. The self that emerges from New Age exercises bears very little likeness to the nature of Christ.

Second, in shadow spirituality the values assigned to all human behavior are rooted in self-justification. There are no absolute standards for right and wrong. Good is what self defines as good. Generally, good is defined as what is beneficial or pleasurable to the self. Evil is what self defines as evil—and generally, that is whatever causes discomfort or bad feelings.

The work of the Holy Spirit is just the opposite. The Spirit reveals that there is no justification for behavior that is contrary to God's commandments. God defines good and evil, and He judges what is right and wrong. God's commands are clearly stated in His Word, and our position is to study God's Word and obey it.

The Holy Spirit Is Involved in Our Forgiveness

When we respond to the Holy Spirit's conviction and confess our sins, it is the Spirit who conveys God's forgiveness to us. *We* confess. *God* forgives. We receive God's forgiveness and then move forward with renewed commitment to obey His commands.

Just as we cannot forgive ourselves, neither do we convict ourselves of the things we need to change. It is our nature to pursue the things that bring pleasure and gratification. It is our fleshly nature to elevate self over God's authority and rule. To address these tendencies, the Holy Spirit opens our eyes to recognize specific personal sins. When He does this convicting work, there is only one acceptable response: to admit our sin, agree with God's assessment that what we have done is wrong, and ask for God's forgiveness.

Forgiveness sets into motion a regenerative work in the human heart and spirit. When God forgives us, He bestows His mercy—an amazing peace, an assurance of His love and acceptance, and tremendous joy at having our relationship with Him restored. It is the Holy Spirit who conveys this wonderful presence of God.

With forgiveness also comes a new desire for God. The Holy Spirit opens our spiritual eyes to understand the Scriptures, opens our minds to comprehend increasingly the depth of God's love, and transforms us into Christ's likeness. The Holy Spirit empowers us to see God's plan and purpose. He empowers us to say no to sinful habits and to say yes to the attitudes and behaviors that bear the character-likeness of Christ Jesus. This work of personal regeneration is a healing work of the Spirit.

2. The Holy Spirit Transforms Us

As the Holy Spirit does the work of glorifying God the Son, He works to transform us into the character-likeness of Christ. This process of spiritual transformation brings tremendous healing to the person who previously had been ripped apart by sin. It's impossible for us to bring about this healing transformation on our own. Only the Holy Spirit can renew our minds and bring us to wholeness.

There are those who have come to faith in Christ after years of diligently seeking the "god within." The more they looked into their own hearts seeking divinity, the greater the darkness they saw there. One person told me,

I was taught that I needed to peel away the layers of myself as if I was peeling away the layers of an onion, and that when I got to the core of my soul, I would discover the meaning and essence of my life. I peeled and peeled away the layers and in the end I found *nothing*. That nothingness was not at all the "nirvana" I had been promised. I had absolutely no feeling of being one with the nothingness of the universe. I just felt *nothing*. I was nothing. I was empty, empty, empty.

This same person said to me several years after allowing the Holy Spirit to do His transforming work in her life:

> In looking at my life, every time I came to a place of horror at my own pain or evil attitudes or bad behavior, the Holy Spirit spoke to me: "Yes, this is something God desires to change in you. I am here to help you make new choices, develop a new attitude, and build a new understanding of who God is, who you are, and how you and God are to relate. For every area of your weakness, I offer you My strength. For every area of your pain, I offer you My comfort. For every area of your doubt, I offer you Jesus Christ and His answer to your longing and need."

She concluded,

> I once was on a quest to peel away myself, layer by layer. I now see the Holy Spirit building me up, layer upon layer. As I make choices to obey God's Word, He empowers me with

the courage and will to do what He commands. I am being remanufactured according to the Owner's manual. I am not in the process of becoming "nothing," but rather I am in the process of being built into someone with whom God wants to spend eternity. I am being made into someone who is more and more like Jesus.

This woman's testimony emphasizes the rule of God in the life of a believer through the transforming work of the Holy Spirit. But not all who call themselves Christians desire to obey His rule. The influence of shadow spirituality is evident in those who claim to be Christians but then attempt to use God to further their own purposes. They attempt to evoke God's presence to transform their lives according to the benefits *they* define, such as better health and greater riches.

They treat the Holy Spirit as if He were their personal slave. They put themselves in charge rather than submitting themselves to the authority of God. Some of these people howl like wolves, hiss like snakes, laugh like drunks, and declare that this is evidence of the Holy Spirit within them. Some breathe on another person and expect the Holy Spirit to knock that person down. Some require money from gullible followers in order to "secure" the Holy Spirit's blessing. These are all examples of a demand being placed upon the Holy Spirit to do man's bidding. Such people could not be more in error.

At no time in the Gospels do we see Jesus manifesting the behaviors these people ascribe to the Holy Spirit. The Holy Spirit's work is to re-shape us more into the likeness of Jesus, and Jesus did not howl, hiss, knock people down, or require money to convey God's blessing.

Those who follow these practices are caught up in false spirituality.

According to God's Word, God defines Himself and makes it clear that we exist to fulfill His purposes. God loves His people, protects them, and blesses them with His presence. But God is never manipulated. We are to walk humbly before Him, seek to obey His just commands, and endeavor to embody His merciful kindness in our dealings with others (see Micah 6:8).

The Humility of the Holy Spirit

Although the Holy Spirit is a Person and is totally God, He is self-effacing—always drawing attention away from Himself to God the Son. The major work of the Holy Spirit is to remind us of what Jesus said and to glorify Him (see John 15:26; 16:14). One way to test whether any manifestation is of the Holy Spirit is to ask, "Does this draw attention to Christ and Christ alone, or does it draw attention to self or some other human?"

Anytime you need to test a spirit or discern the motives of a person or institution, ask yourself: "Who or what is being glorified?" If all the glory is going to the Lord Jesus, then the Holy Spirit is at work. If honor, praise, or reward is being directed to any person or any thing other than Christ Jesus, a spirit other than the Holy Spirit is at work.

Our world is quick to proclaim, "It's all about me." This is the very antithesis of the Holy Spirit's proclamation: "It's all about Jesus." The world's avoidance of the name of Jesus is pervasive. It is acceptable to speak publicly about God or to evoke a higher power, a supreme being, or a "life force." To speak the name of Jesus Christ, however, is not acceptable. To pray in the name of God is permissible, but to pray in the name of Jesus is not.

I have seen this across the United States and also in Asia, Europe, and the Middle East. Sadly, a number of Christian leaders have given in to the pressure and have refused to pray publicly in the name of Jesus. Why the strong resistance to a prayer in Jesus' name? Most unbelievers do not believe God is a Person. They view Him instead as a nebulous and rather benign "force." Jesus, on the other hand, is far too personal and far too potent. That is why His name is banned from public expression.

Many people believe in man rather than in God. So when they refer to "god," they are actually referring to themselves. In the same way, many people are happy to talk about the "spirit," but they most certainly are not referring to the Holy Spirit of Almighty God.

3. The Holy Spirit Seals Us as God's Own

A third major teaching in the Scriptures about the Holy Spirit is this: The Holy Spirit "seals" believers (see 2 Corinthians 1:22; Ephesians 1:13; 4:30). The sealing of the Holy Spirit is not something we experience. It's simply a factual reality that occurs in heaven, regardless of how we may "feel" on earth.

If this makes no difference to our experience of everyday life, why is it important to us? It's important for three reasons, each having to do with the biblical meaning of a seal, and each one providing a wonderful metaphor for the healing work of the Holy Spirit.

A Stamp of Ownership

In ancient times as well as today, when a property contract is finalized, the new owner signs it or places his seal upon it to declare that the transaction is complete and the property is now under his ownership. When the Holy Spirit enters a person's life, He puts God's seal or stamp of ownership on that person. He declares now and forever that we belong to God. In so doing, the Holy Spirit elevates our worth beyond comparison.

Somebody once paid $21,000 for Napoleon's used toothbrush. Another paid $150,000 for Hitler's used automobile. And thousands of dollars were paid for C. S. Lewis's used pipe. Sotheby's Auction House sold Jackie Kennedy Onassis's *fake* pearls for $211,500 and President John F. Kennedy's used golf clubs for $772,500. As new products sold in a store, these items never would have gone for hundreds of thousands of dollars. The auctioned items were valuable because of who owned them.

The same is true for us. We become infinitely valuable—beyond any monetary measure—because of who owns us. God the Father paid the highest price possible, the life of His only Son, for our salvation. God the Son died in our place so we would not have to die in sin. Our worth has nothing to do with what we have done, achieved, or acquired. Our worth has everything to do with what Christ Jesus did on the cross on our behalf.

John Calvin wrote:

> We are not our own.... We are God's; let us, therefore, live
> and die.... We are God's; to him, then, as the only legiti-
> mate end, let every part of our life be directed. We are not
> our own; therefore, as far as possible, let us forget ourselves
> and the things that are ours.... We are God's; let us, there-
> fore, live, and die to him.[1]

The Holy Spirit "seals" us with ownership the moment we declare our belief in Jesus as Savior and place our trust in Him. As believers, we are God's permanent possessions.

A Sign of Security in Christ

When the Holy Spirit seals us, He guarantees that our status as God's own will never change. Because the seal of the Holy Spirit is secure, our salvation is sure.

True spirituality does not immunize Christians from Satan's attacks. Satan continues to try to mire believers in sin. The world constantly pulls at us to pursue our natural lusts. We often wander away from the Lord and grieve the Holy Spirit. No matter what pulls at us, however, the Holy Spirit's seal remains tight. We rest securely in Christ because His Spirit resides in us.

The Spirit's sealing has nothing to do with our changeable feelings and emotions or our misbehavior. The sealing of our lives occurs in heaven, out of the reach of both man and Satan. The seal is so secure that the apostle Paul wrote that, in some cases, God has even taken the lives of Christians who persist in disobeying and dishonoring Him on earth rather than allow them to continue in their sin (see 1 Corinthians 11:30). The security of the believer is not up for grabs—it is guaranteed by God. Consider the testimony of the apostle Paul:

> I am convinced that neither death nor life, neither angels
> nor demons, neither the present nor the future, nor any
> powers, neither height nor depth, nor anything else in all
> creation, will be able to separate us from the love of God
> that is in Christ Jesus our Lord. (Romans 8:38-39)

A Sign of Authenticity

The Holy Spirit's seal upon us is a sign of authenticity that the spiritual work that God has done in our lives is real, lasting, and of the highest value. Merchants in the ancient seaport of Ephesus placed their seal on the high-quality timber they sold so that their lumber would not be confused with inferior grades of wood. Buyers looked for that mark of authenticity before they purchased timber. In a similar manner God puts His seal of ownership on us by placing the Holy Spirit in us. He identifies us and authenticates us as children of God.

What does this mean to those who pursue true spirituality? It means that anytime Satan tries to make us doubt whether we are authentically claimed by Christ Jesus, the Holy Spirit is our inner witness that, indeed, we belong to Christ. It is the Holy Spirit who enables us to say, "I have repented of my sin. I have received Jesus as my Savior and Lord. The Holy Spirit lives within me and authenticates my faith. I believe this because God's Word says it is so. In the name of Jesus, be gone, and take your doubts with you!" God's Word declares that the Holy Spirit gives witness to our spirits that we *are* the sons and daughters of God (see Romans 8:16).

4. The Holy Spirit Fills Us with His Presence

The Bible shows us a fourth essential truth about the Holy Spirit: He continuously fills our lives so we might experience His presence and power. This ongoing "filling" of our lives with God's Spirit is the essence of our day-to-day spirituality.

While the sealing of the Holy Spirit happens only once—at the time of our surrender to Him—the "filling" of our lives with God's Spirit is something that can and should happen every moment of every day. This filling is dependent upon our response to God's gracious gift of salvation and our desire to obey Jesus as our Lord. As we are filled, God's Spirit guides us, admonishes us, corrects us, comforts us, and leads us away from evil and toward the good plans and purposes that our heavenly Father has for us.

Every Christian is sealed by the Holy Spirit, but not every believing Christian chooses to be filled or led daily by the Holy Spirit. God the Holy Spirit does not overpower us with His presence and power. He waits for us to open ourselves to Him and yield our wills to His will. It is our responsibility and privilege every day to *invite* the Holy Spirit to do His work in us and through us.

Let me be very clear on one aspect of the Spirit's filling. At the time of salvation, a person receives the *whole* of the person of the Holy Spirit, not just part of Him. When asked, "How much of the Holy Spirit have you received?" the answer is always, "*All* of the Holy Spirit."

The more important questions to ask are these: How much are you allowing the Holy Spirit to fill every part of your life every day? Have you yielded *all* of your life to the working of the Holy Spirit, or have you cornered His presence and power into one small area of your life?

The sealing of the Holy Spirit does not depend on our cooperation. We stretch out our hands by faith and receive His ownership, security, and authentication of our lives. The *filling* of the Holy Spirit, in contrast, is an ongoing act of cooperation—it is a continuous yielding and submission of our will and our desires to the Holy Spirit's guidance.

The apostle Paul wrote, "Be filled with the Spirit" (Ephesians 5:18). The Greek word in this sentence for *be filled* actually means "be constantly or continually filled."

We live in the healing power of the Holy Spirit when we are continually filled with Him. But how can we receive this filling every day, and with what does He fill us? Those are the questions at the heart of the next chapter.

Three

UNDERSTANDING THE
SPIRIT'S POWER

Finding the Key to Our Ongoing Spirituality

What better description of the Holy Spirit could we have than that used by Jesus? When the Son of God spoke of the Holy Spirit, He referred to the Spirit of God as the divine *Paraclete*. There is no equivalent word in the English language. The Greek word *paraclete* conveys a number of meanings, including "comforter, helper, supporter, advisor, advocate, ally, mature friend, and giver of strength."

Could there be a better description of Jesus as He walked and taught and performed miracles on this earth? Could there be a more complete description of Jesus as He lived in close association with His disciples? In telling His disciples that He would be sending the Paraclete to them, Jesus was saying, "I am going to send you a Person just like Me!"

The apostle Paul wrote to the Corinthians:

> He [the Lord] said to me, "My grace is sufficient for you,
> for my power is made perfect in weakness." Therefore I will
> boast all the more gladly about my weaknesses, so that
> Christ's power may rest on me. That is why, for Christ's

sake, I delight in weaknesses, in insults, in hardships, in persecutions, in difficulties. For when I am weak, then I am strong. (2 Corinthians 12:9-10)

Even as he languished in the bowels of a prison, Paul could write, "I can do everything through him who gives me strength" (Philippians 4:13). In his own power Paul felt pain, sorrow, and need. With God's power flowing in and through him, he felt joy, contentment, and peace. God's presence and all that He represents—His truth, comfort, and wisdom—cannot be separated from God's power. Very simply, His presence is powerful. His presence transforms us. Indeed, being in His presence heals us.

Jesus didn't want His disciples to be unaware of the power that the Holy Spirit brings, so he told them: "You will receive power when the Holy Spirit comes on you; and you will be my witnesses in Jerusalem, and in all Judea and Samaria, and to the ends of the earth" (Acts 1:8). And in another reference to the Spirit's power, He said: "I am going to send you what my Father has promised; but stay in the city until you have been clothed with power from on high" (Luke 24:49). Those who received the Holy Spirit lived their daily lives and conducted the work of their ministries with supernatural power (see Acts 6:8).

GOD'S VIEW OF POWER

When we speak of the power of the Holy Spirit, many people—even Christians—misunderstand the term *power*. They tend to define power as the world defines it. And most believers appear to pursue power in the same way the world pursues it.

In the world's view, power conveys the ability to control people, events, and circumstances. The world's power is used to manipulate others to get what is desired, and it elevates the "powerful" above their enemies and detractors. In the world, power brings with it a high degree of independence and self-sufficiency, with no need for the help of others.

While many devote their lives to achieving this sort of power, let me assure you that this type of power cannot last. It can never satisfy the soul or bring joy or peace. The world's power is temporary, leaving a person always wanting more. It never operates out of love for others. No one who pursues the power advocated by the world can find genuine fulfillment or a purpose beyond self.

The Bible, in describing the power of the Holy Spirit, paints quite a different picture (see Luke 24:49; Acts 1:8; 2 Corinthians 12:9). The word translated as *power* in the English Bible is the Greek work *dynamis,* from which we get the word *dynamite.* In Acts 1:8, Jesus told His disciples that before they would be able to evangelize the world, they must receive the *dynamis* of the Holy Spirit.

The Holy Spirit possesses a dynamite-like power that works within a believer to blast out anything that is unlike God. It is not a power that exalts one person above others. It does not manipulate or control others, and it does not enable a person to become independent of others. The Holy Spirit uses His power to break us so that He might remake us.

To experience the power of the Holy Spirit, we must acknowledge our utter helplessness and our complete dependence on God. It is in the most humble of hearts that God shows Himself strongest. It is in the life that is broken in surrender and worship before the Lord that God reveals His greatest power. It is in the life that is totally submitted to His will that God manifests Himself fully able to meet every need.

The Holy Spirit does not make us powerful people. Rather, He works in us and through us as vessels of His work in the world. The more we get self out of the way and yield our will to His, the more powerfully He is able to pour Himself through us to others, and the more powerfully He is able to transform our lives. The power is His; we are only the conduits.

God the Holy Spirit displays His omnipotence in the weak and the despised. The power of the Holy Spirit is, and always remains, His own. This power is never made available for our selfish use. It does not draw attention to self, promote self, or manipulate others. When we attempt to misuse His power, the Holy Spirit withdraws His power from us.

The Holy Spirit empowers us to witness of God's love, to live in a way that pleases God, to meet fully the demands and pressures of life, and to fight temptation. The power of the Holy Spirit is the only power that is sufficient to win spiritual battles against the minions of Satan.

THOSE WHO RECEIVE THE SPIRIT'S POWER

Just as it is possible for us to disobey God even when His will for us is abundantly clear, it is also possible for us to live in such a way that the Holy Spirit withholds His power from our lives. So how can we put ourselves in a position to experience the Spirit's power?

Admit Weakness

We put ourselves in position to receive God's power when we become realistic about our limitations and inadequacies. Even the apostle Paul, who accomplished so much for the gospel, asked in his letter to the Corinthians, "Who is equal to such a task?" (2 Corinthians 2:16).

The key to spiritual power is the exact opposite of striving for success and seeking to promote ourselves. Instead, the key is humility. God honors those with broken spirits who are utterly dependent on Him. God manifests His power in those who lay their weakness at His feet. Whenever I am tempted to believe that I'm responsible for some breakthrough in our ministry, I remember the many times I have felt completely overwhelmed by the demands and the difficulty of living for God. During the times when I am physically worn out and feel inadequate in my ministry, I find comfort in this apocryphal story:

> As Jesus walked along a road, He came to a man who was crying. Jesus asked him, "Friend, what is wrong?" The man said, "I am blind." The Lord restored his sight.
>
> Jesus continued on His journey and came upon another man who was crying. He asked the man, "Friend, what is wrong?" The man replied, "I am lame. I cannot walk." Jesus raised him up and enabled him to walk again.
>
> Jesus hadn't gone much farther before he came to another crying man. Again, He said, "Friend, what's wrong?" The man said, "I am a pastor." And Jesus sat down and cried with him.

As a pastor I often have found myself crying, "Lord, help me. Lord, strengthen me. Lord, enable me. Lord, give me your power!" What am I really asking for? I want the power of the Lord so I can witness with boldness and effectiveness. I want the power to live in a way that is 100 percent pleasing to God. I want God's power to make me equal to the demands and pressures I face, to fight temptation, and to experience victory over sin. I want God's power working in my life to defeat the spiritual Enemy who continually seeks to bring about loss, destruction, and an end to blessing in my life (see John 10:10).

In seeking God's power to bring about these works, I am seeking the same things that all who deeply desire to follow the Lord Jesus seek. In my own strength I will surely be defeated. But in the strength of the Holy Spirit, I am in position to be more than a conqueror (see Romans 8:37).

Avoid the Traps

The second way we put ourselves in position to experience the power of the Holy Spirit is to avoid power-related traps. One of the most common is to downplay the power of the Holy Spirit and fail to seek it in our lives. Many Christians have reacted against the excessive, show-business atmosphere that surrounds those who make a great display of exercising "spiritual power." These theatrical demonstrations have caused believers to close themselves to the authentic power of the Holy Spirit.

Another trap is a simple lack of belief. There are many who acknowledge the Holy Spirit's existence but live as if His presence in their lives is an option rather than a necessity. The end result is that they live and act as if there were no Holy Spirit, and in so doing, they fail to experience the guidance and comfort that come through His presence with us.

A common and very tempting trap is to seek the Holy Spirit only for His power. If a person desires power so that his own needs will be met, he will not receive it. The power of the Holy Spirit is given so we might use it to bless others. God's power is never meant for the exclusive use of any one person.

Among Christians, a frequent mistake is to seek the power of the Spirit as a substitute for faithfully practicing the spiritual disciplines. These believers sit quietly and wait for God's power to overtake them so they won't have to bother studying God's Word, spending hours with the Lord in prayer, or getting involved in service to others. They see the power of the Spirit as an easy route to spiritual maturity, which is never what God has promised.

Too many people say such things as: "I'm just waiting for God to carry me along"…"I don't have to do a thing, I'll let God do it all"…"I will just sit and wait for God's power to motivate me." When people do this, they are looking for magic. In the end they are attempting to use God as an excuse for their own lack of faith and discipline.

Another significant mistake is the expectation that a dose of God's power will remove all unpleasantness, temptation, or struggle from life. That simply is not the case. The power of the Holy Spirit enables us to *withstand* evil and temptation and to *persevere* in times of persecution or hardship, but the power of the Holy Spirit is never a vaccination against difficulty.

I can assure you from my own walk with the Lord that life is a daily fight against the push and pull of the world. Life is a daily battle against temptation. It is a daily struggle against countless forces that seek to destroy our health, finances, emotional well-being, families, friendships, and the preaching of the gospel. God gives us His Spirit to help us endure and overcome in difficult times, but His Spirit does not prevent difficulties from coming our way.

One last trap is the habit of beating ourselves up with feelings of inadequacy and lack of faith whenever things do not turn out as *we* desire. God's Spirit at work in us does not mean that we will never get sick. He does not always protect us from accidents or natural catastrophes. Too many believers think that if they have more faith or if they have more of the Holy Spirit, they will have perfect lives. That is not what God promises. But He does assure us of this: *I will be with you.* We err greatly when we beat ourselves up with guilt for not being "spiritual enough."

When we focus on our own inadequacy, we turn the spotlight on self rather than on God. We focus on our own struggles more than God's sufficiency. We focus on the difficulty of the battle rather than on the victory of God. When we do this, we become morbid, gloomy people, and as we wallow in our failures, we give no opportunity for the Spirit of God to do His work in us and through us.

God the Holy Spirit desires for us to be joyous Christians. He wants us to walk in the power of the Spirit and allow the Holy Spirit to nurture and strengthen our relationship with God the Father and Jesus the Son. He wants to help us become faithful followers of Christ Jesus, living righteous lives in a wicked world, not apart from the world. He wants to reveal His adequacy for all of our inadequacies.

THE PROBLEM OF SELF

There are any number of ways we can cheat ourselves out of experiencing the healing power of the Holy Spirit. And most of them are problems closely related to self.

The pride that inhabits the self convinces us that we don't need the Holy Spirit. Our self seeks power for selfish glory. The self is lazy and refuses to take responsibility for the things God has clearly made us responsible for. At other times, the self tries to take responsibility for things that God is clearly in charge of.

Self, self, self. We must remind ourselves continually, "I belong to God. I live and move and have my being in Him. He is the Lord of my life. He is the Maker of all that I am. I am a vessel in His hands."

One of the techniques my parents used to keep me in check as a young teen was to remind me often, "Remember our good and godly family name." At times I resented their saying this. But I realize now that my parents' frequent reminders that I was a Youssef kept me from a whole lot of trouble!

We need to remember who resides within us. We need to remind ourselves whose we are. We need always to focus on the One who gives us the power to avoid sin, gives us the power to receive the fullness of God's provision for us, and gives us the power to discern His will and do it.

Don't focus on what you can't do. Focus instead on what God can do for you and through you in the lives of others. Have faith that He works *all* things to your eternal good (see Romans 8:28).

If God is your Father, then you are His child, a member of His family. Every day remember to whom you belong!

Four

How God's Spirit Makes Us Whole

The Holy Spirit Fills Us to Bear Fruit

D. L. Moody once stood before a group of students with an empty glass in his hand. He asked the students, "How do I get the air out of this glass?" The students came up with a variety of suggestions on how to create a vacuum inside the glass, but they could never get beyond the fact that in removing the air from the glass, it would implode and shatter.

Finally, Moody reached for a pitcher and filled the glass with water. The liquid displaced the air, causing no damage to the glass.

The famous evangelist could just as easily have stood before the students and asked, "How can I remove all the things within me that do not glorify God?"

The answer is not to come up with clever strategies or some new technology that could selectively remove the bad while leaving everything else unharmed. No, the answer is that we must be filled with something else. Only when we allow the Holy Spirit to fill us completely are we empowered and enabled to live without sinning.

God's Word says:

No one who is born of God will continue to sin, because
God's seed remains in him; he cannot go on sinning,
because he has been born of God. This is how we know
who the children of God are and who the children of the
devil are: Anyone who does not do what is right is not a
child of God; nor is anyone who does not love his brother.
(1 John 3:9-10)

Can we really live without sin? The Holy Spirit, who dwells within
every believer, can enable us to live in a sinful world and yet not participate in the sin of the world.

REMOVING THE HINDRANCES

Anyone who has helped create a hiking trail through a forest—and for
that matter, any person who has ever worked in construction—knows
that the first job in building a trail, a road, or a new neighborhood is
to clear the area. Boulders and trees and stumps and all sorts of other
obstacles must be removed. In our lives, a choice to be truly spiritual
also involves the removal of two main hindrances to the Spirit's work.
God's Word refers to these hindrances as quenching the Spirit (see
1 Thessalonians 5:19, NKJV) and grieving the Holy Spirit (see Ephesians
4:30).

For a Christian to be filled with the Holy Spirit, she must remove
these two hindrances. In fact, the New Testament has fourteen references
to our being filled with the Spirit, and every one of them has conditions
attached to it.

Do Not Quench the Holy Spirit

The Greek word that is translated as *quench* means "to extinguish." Picture a soft drink commercial selling a beverage that promises to quench your thirst. We all know that a cold drink on a hot day will do just that. Our thirst does not disappear forever, but it is suppressed for the moment.

The Greek word for *quench* has a stronger meaning than "temporary suppression." It means "to extinguish, snuff out, or put an end to." One modern Bible translation says, "Do not put out the Spirit's fire" (1 Thessalonians 5:19, NIV). The same word is used to describe the snuffing of a candle.

This does not mean that we can permanently remove the Holy Spirit from our lives. It is not possible to *fully* extinguish the Holy Spirit once we become a child of God. Likewise, no one can extinguish the Holy Spirit in another person's life. The Holy Spirit is indestructible in His Person and inextinguishable in His effect.

Rather, it means that we can resist something the Holy Spirit wants to do in us or through us to the point that His work will not occur. The Holy Spirit will not force His will upon us. Through the exercise of free will, we can put a stop to the work of the Holy Spirit in our personal lives and in our corporate lives as a church. Quenching the Holy Spirit is refusing to follow His leading. It is ignoring His warnings and charging ahead to do things our way and in our own timing.

Quenching the Holy Spirit is an act of rebellion, but the level of this rebellion isn't always obvious to us. Consider the believer who uses all his energy to cater to his own needs and spends all his money on himself. God the Holy Spirit says to that person, "I want you to inconvenience yourself, to take time from caring for yourself to pray for somebody else."

The person responds, "Oh yes. I need to do that. I should do that," but then he does nothing.

The Holy Spirit speaks again, giving the same directives. The person says, "Yes, yes. I have got to do that," but then he gets busy with other things and does nothing.

The Holy Spirit speaks yet again. And each time the person hears His voice, he says "yes, yes," but does nothing.

Eventually, the person is so accustomed to saying yes, while doing nothing, that he no longer senses the Holy Spirit's stirring. By not doing what he knows he should do, he has quenched the Spirit of God.

We all come to a crossroads where we have the opportunity to yield to the Holy Spirit or to quench the Spirit's work in us. We may sense that we are to serve in some way, to give money to meet a need, or to change a destructive habit. To quench the Spirit is to say no to the Lord in these moments, to refuse to heed His voice, and to choose instead to do what *we* want to do to achieve our personal goals or comfort. Quenching the Holy Spirit means ignoring or deliberately disobeying the leading of God to do something that is not self-serving but God-serving.

We can choose to disregard the "still small voice" that encourages, challenges, or compels us to act outside ourselves for service to God and others or that speaks to us about a particular habit or error in our lives that God wants to change.

The story is told of a young man who went to see a psychologist at a college counseling center. He said to the therapist, "Doc, I have no self-control. I often find myself doing the wrong thing, and my conscience is bothering me."

The counselor responded, "So you want something that will strengthen your willpower?"

The young man replied, "Oh no. I'd rather you tell me how to weaken my conscience."

The net effect of quenching the Holy Spirit is very often a hardening or weakening of our conscience.

Many times, quenching the Holy Spirit is related to areas in which the Bible does not give clear commandments. For example, there is nothing in the Bible that says, "Thou shalt serve in the children's ministry at church, or be part of a prayer team, or get involved in an outreach on a college campus." Nevertheless, the Holy Spirit may be speaking in the heart of a believer, "I want you to do this. This is the area in which I want you to serve Me."

Christians play all sorts of self-justification games as they quench the Holy Spirit. They often say to the Lord: "I'm not worthy of this place of service. I'm sure there is somebody more qualified than I am who will step in and do this much better than I could."

Believers often use the excuse of busyness to resist the people the Holy Spirit uses to confirm His call on their lives. "God has given me lots to do right now," a person will say as she quenches the Spirit. "I'll participate in that ministry opportunity when some of my other obligations are fulfilled."

The truth, however, is that the Holy Spirit will never call a person to do something unless He *expects* that person to obey. God never waits for us to be "worthy" or "qualified" or to have sufficient spare time for ministry. He assures us that He will make us strong in areas where we are weak, He will equip us and qualify us by His presence, and He is the Lord over all our time and obligations.

Along with listening for His voice, a primary condition for being filled with the Holy Spirit is to be willing to do what He commands. The ultimate example of a person *not* quenching the Holy Spirit is Jesus as He cried out in the Garden of Gethsemane, "Not my will, but yours" (see Matthew 26:39). That is the ultimate expression of obeying what the Holy Spirit compels us to do.

To break a habit of quenching the Spirit, we must immediately say yes to God whenever and wherever He leads. We must admit to the Lord that we have shut Him out and resisted His plan, and we must tell Him we are submitting our lives anew to His guidance.

Do Not Grieve the Holy Spirit

The second condition that must be met for us to be filled with the Holy Spirit is to avoid grieving Him (see Ephesians 4:30). We grieve the Holy Spirit by sinning. We grieve the Spirit by blatantly choosing to disobey God's desires. Consider a believer who lies, cheats, or commits adultery, all the while knowing that the Word of God clearly says this is a sin. And he does this not once, but repeatedly. That believer is grieving the Holy Spirit.

We grieve the Holy Spirit of God by disobeying clear commandments in Scripture. We grieve the Holy Spirit by our repeated, habitual sins that become a lifestyle of sinning. We grieve the Holy Spirit when we repeatedly ignore any of God's commandments, choosing instead to make up our own rules.

The Sin That Grieves the Spirit

The sin that grieves the Holy Spirit is not an error or a misjudgment or even an action of rebellion that results in remorse and immediate repentance. It is constant and continuous sin—it is knowingly living in habitual sin. Christians have an amazing ability to rationalize their sin. One might say: "Everybody is doing it, and God isn't striking people down, so He must not think this sin is all that terrible." Or they might try to justify their behavior: "God made me, so He must have given me this propensity to sin. I just can't help the way I was made."

Wrong on all counts. The Holy Spirit reveals to us that we are choosing something contrary to God's plan, purpose, and commandments. The Holy Spirit confirms to us that *all* sin is an offense against the Lord—all sin has terrible consequences and ultimately can result in our death. The Holy Spirit says to us that we don't have any desire or weakness that is beyond God's ability to heal and redirect. The more we deny the truth of what the Holy Spirit declares in our heart, the more we grieve Him.

When I grieve the Holy Spirit, He is not able to give me power to find peace and purpose in life. The Holy Spirit never ignores sin or dismisses it as trivial. In the long run the Spirit will not bless us—spiritually, emotionally, relationally, or materially—when we choose to disregard God's Word. When we grieve the Holy Spirit, He withdraws His power and His blessing.

The Remedy

There is one solution to the sin of grieving the Spirit, and that is the act of confession. God tells us, "If we confess our sins, he is faithful and just and will forgive us our sins and purify us from all unrighteousness" (1 John 1:9). Confession and forgiveness of sin remove the barrier between ourselves and the Holy Spirit. Until true confession takes place, our relationship with God cannot be restored.

Confession requires self-judgment. According to 1 Corinthians 11:31, "If we judged ourselves, we would not come under judgment." Before we can or will confess, we first must recognize that what we are doing is wrong. We must say, "I admit to myself that I am in error before God," before we can arrive at the place of saying to the Lord, "I admit to You, Lord, that I have sinned."

But how are we to know that we have sinned? Not only do we feel the conviction of having sinned, but we also have been given the mirror of God's Word. The Scriptures make clear what God approves and disapproves, what God commands, what God requires, what God blesses. We need to read the Word, study it, apply it, and ask the Holy Spirit daily to reveal to us the truth of God so we might live in it.

Producing the Fruit of the Spirit

When we are sealed by the Holy Spirit and experience the moment-by-moment filling of the Spirit, we begin to bear the fruit of the Spirit. We begin to manifest the outworking, or the results, of the Holy Spirit's presence. His work is manifested in our thoughts and emotions and in our behavior toward others.

If you have ever watched the harvesting of grapes, you know that two people usually work together. One person holds an open basket or box while the other person cuts the grapes and lays the clusters into the container. As long as the person with the basket keeps the basket open and follows closely along with the cutter, her fruit basket will soon be filled to overflowing. But if her basket closes or she lags behind, she does not receive the fruit.

In a similar way, as long as a person is walking closely connected to the Lord and is keeping his life open to receive the daily filling of the Holy Spirit, he will see his life filled with the fruit of the Spirit. The fruit of the Spirit is character rather than conduct; it is being rather than doing. The "fruit" is the likeness of the Holy Spirit. It is the quality and nature of His life imparted to us. Many people mistakenly refer to the "fruits" of the Spirit, as if they could be separated out and accepted or rejected individually. Let me quickly dispel this notion. The fruit of the Spirit is a single fruit, not an assortment of fruits. The fruit of the Spirit is the *whole* of God's nature imparted to us and flowing out of us as evidence that the Spirit resides in us.

Those who claim to be Spirit-filled but evidence no spiritual fruit are faking it. To have Christ as Savior is to have the Holy Spirit resident within. To have the Holy Spirit is to have the opportunity to be filled daily with the Spirit. To be filled daily with the Spirit is to manifest His nature, to bear His fruit.

Those who claim that they have a few of the character traits of the Spirit but not the others don't understand that God's nature is not fragmented. We cannot receive just one aspect of His being. And we must not attempt to pick and choose the character traits of God as if we were shopping for produce at the supermarket. We bear *all* the fruit of the Spirit, not *some* fruit.

The composite nature of God's character is summarized by the apostle Paul in his letter to the Galatians: "love, joy, peace, patience, kindness, goodness, faithfulness, gentleness [meekness] and self-control" (Galatians 5:22-23). This description of God's character also describes the fruit that the Holy Spirit bears in our lives.

GOD AT WORK IN US

The outworking of the Holy Spirit is not something that we can manufacture. It is His work alone.

The story is told of two young brothers who were experts at making good use of a fruit tree that grew just outside their upstairs bedroom. They loved the tree, not for its fruit, but for the close proximity of its limbs to their bedroom window. When they were sent to their room as a punishment, they would climb out the window, scurry down the tree, and continue to play outside. When it came time for dinner, they would climb back up the tree and go into their room, all the while trying to keep their behavior a secret from their parents.

One day their father announced that he was going to cut down the tree because it never produced fruit. Not wanting their ladder to freedom taken away, the boys rushed to the grocery store, bought a sack of apples, and returned home, where they scattered the apples under the tree. The next day their father saw the apples and expressed his amazement. "It's a miracle," he proclaimed, "that this pear tree has produced apples!"

In a sincere desire to attain the signs of spirituality, many people are spreading apples under pear trees. They are trying to produce spiritual fruit on their own. Let me assure you, if there's one thing that cannot be faked, it is true spirituality.

Bearing fruit is not a self-improvement program. We cannot talk ourselves into developing these character traits. We cannot study our way into them, motivate our way into them, or discipline our way into them. They are the by-product of our allowing the Holy Spirit to do His work in us as we abide in the words of Christ Jesus, obey the commands of Christ, and follow the leading of the Holy Spirit to carry out what He calls us to do.

Furthermore, no other person can produce fruit in us. No matter what a person proclaims over us, prophesies over us, prays over us, preaches to us, or nags at us to do…that person cannot produce in us the character-likeness of Christ. The fruit of the Spirit is born only when the Spirit Himself indwells and fills the life of the believer.

WHAT IT MEANS TO ABIDE

What is our part in the fruit-bearing process? Staying connected to the Holy Spirit. We are commanded by Jesus to "abide" in Him, to rest in Him, to rely upon Him, to trust Him, to resort to Him at every turn and when facing every decision. Abiding is becoming so connected to Him that we no longer can tell where our will ends and His begins.

Jesus taught His disciples:

> I am the vine; you are the branches. If a man remains in me
> and I in him, he will bear much fruit; apart from me you
> can do nothing. If anyone does not remain in me, he is like
> a branch that is thrown away and withers; such branches are
> picked up, thrown into the fire and burned. If you remain
> in me and my words remain in you, ask whatever you wish,
> and it will be given you. This is to my Father's glory, that
> you bear much fruit, showing yourselves to be my disciples.
> (John 15:5-8)

If you leave a branch attached to a healthy grapevine, it naturally will bear grapes. True spirituality works the same way. As we remain connected to God's Son through the power of the indwelling Holy Spirit, we will naturally bear spiritual fruit—the evidence of true spirituality. If we are separate from Him—or if we separate ourselves from Him through dis-obedience—then we can no more produce spiritual fruit than a dead branch cut off from the grapevine can produce grapes.

GOD'S CHARACTER IN US

We listed the nine attributes of the Holy Spirit's nature earlier: love, joy, peace, patience, kindness, goodness, faithfulness, gentleness [meekness], and self-control (see Galatians 5:22-23). These character traits of Christ are the character traits the Holy Spirit desires to create in us. They form the composite nature that the Holy Spirit seeks to manifest through us.

How can you tell if you have these character traits? The best test is the "squeeze test." We've all heard the expression: "What do you get when you squeeze a lemon? Lemon juice!" Likewise, what character do you display when you are under great stress? The best time to determine a person's true character is when she is under stress. Someone once said, "Christians are like tea bags. Their strength can only be manifested when they are in hot water."

A person may manifest certain character traits when things are going well, when life is flowing smoothly, when those around her are loving and generous and kind. But put that person in a difficult situation, and you will see her *true* character traits come out. People may live for brief moments in a protected hothouse environment, where fruit grows easily. But most of life is problem-filled, with tough choices and challenges, hard circumstances and difficult demands, crises and mundane obligations that sap our energy. It is when the pressures of life threaten to crush us that we display who we truly are. At those times, if we don't like what we see, we must ask, "Am I connected to the Spirit? If not, why not?"

If you are like me, as you read the description of the Spirit's fruit—the character qualities manifested by the Holy Spirit—you are likely to throw up your hands and cry, "That's an impossible standard!" That's the point. You can't bear the fruit of the Spirit in your own strength. These character traits can only be manifested in you by the Holy Spirit, who fills you daily with His presence and power. It is in yielding our empty selves to Him—readily admitting that in our own power we are not loving, not joyful, not at peace, not patient, not faithful, not kind, not good, not meek, not self-controlled and crying out to Him for more of His presence and His help—that He fills us with the character-likeness of Christ.

To be filled with the Spirit means first to be emptied of self. To become more like Him, we must become less bound to our own impulses and desires. How this happens is a great mystery of God, but it is undeniably true nonetheless. It is the fruit that comes from living a genuine spiritual life that results in our wholeness and fulfillment.

A SERIES OF CHOICES

Anyone who seeks to become a biblically spiritual person must make a series of choices. In light of God's character, we must honestly answer these questions:

- Am I going to pursue the temporary, false spirituality that the world offers, or am I going to pursue true spirituality?
- Have I repented of my sin and accepted Jesus Christ as my Savior and Lord?
- Am I asking the Holy Spirit to control my life moment by moment? Do I come to Him daily in brokenness and humility and utter dependence?

- Am I quenching the Spirit by disregarding His directives or grieving the Spirit by not obeying His Word? When I become aware that I have quenched or grieved the Holy Spirit, do I immediately confess my fault to God and ask for His forgiveness?
- When life's difficulties arise, do I ask God to use them to produce His fruit in me? Do I daily seek for the Spirit's fruit to be borne in my life?

Your honest answers to these questions will determine if you are pursuing genuine spirituality and are becoming more like Christ. Your answers determine the degree to which you are experiencing the spirituality that can heal you from the inside out and make you whole.

As we take a closer look at the fruit of the Holy Spirit in the chapters that follow, think about these questions and your responses. Ask God to help you submit all of your being to His rule so that your life may manifest the character of Christ that is produced in you through the Spirit's fruit.

Five

THE HEALING POWER
OF GOD'S LOVE

Trading Self-Centeredness for God's Unconditional Love

Perhaps the most abused, misused, and wrongly overused word in the English language is *love.*

Some parents refuse to discipline and train their children, and they call their permissiveness love. Some husbands and wives refuse to be honest and open with each other, and they call their lack of forthrightness love. Some couples move in together, refusing to make the commitment of marriage, and they call their immorality love. Friends often fail to speak the truth to each other, and they say they do this out of love.

All kinds of lusts and selfishness are presented to us on television and movie screens in the name of love. Entire church denominations refuse to identify unbiblical actions as sin, and they make that decision out of so-called love. There has never been a time when the concept of love has been more confused than in our time. Some cynics define love as "what happens between a man and woman who don't know each other." Another has claimed that love is "temporary insanity—curable by marriage."

The story is told of a young man who proposed to his girlfriend. As they sat together looking out at a beautiful lake, he said, "Darling, I want you to know that I love you more than anything in the world. I want you to marry me. I'm not wealthy. I don't have a yacht or a Rolls-Royce like Johnny Brown. But I do love you with all my heart."

The young woman responded, "I love you, too, with all my heart. But tell me more about Johnny Brown."

In July 1999 the city of Berlin attracted 1.5 million young people to what was advertised as a "love fest." When one of the organizers was asked, "Would it not be more accurate to call it 'lust fest'?" the organizer replied, "That is what it is, but calling it 'love fest' sounds much better."

Oscar Wilde, a hedonistic British playwright, once stated, "To love oneself...is the beginning of a life-long romance."[1]

Positive-thinking preacher Robert Schuller has said that to love oneself is to be truly religious.[2]

Newsweek columnist Gary Wills has written: "The importance of feeling good about oneself...has become a national and personal priority. It has become a patriotic, even religious duty."[3]

A major heresy of recent years is that unless people love themselves and believe they are worthy of God's love, they will never come to Christ. The shadow spirituality of the New Age movement contends that it is only as we love ourselves that we are able to open our eyes and hearts to receive God's unconditional love. Sadly, this belief is also held by many in the modern church. But it is the exact opposite of God's truth. We come to Christ when we recognize that we are *nothing* without God, and that even in our sinful state, Christ died for us. The person who is absorbed with self-love sees no need for God.

It is in the midst of this utter distortion of the meaning of that beautiful word *love* that true spirituality can heal us. We are all starving for a personal experience of genuine, biblical love.

GOD'S UNCONDITIONAL LOVE

True love does not occur apart from God, and for the follower of God, love is not optional. That is because God's love flows from His nature. It is His nature to love—as John wrote, "God is love" (1 John 4:8). His character is defined by love. God has made an eternal choice from the foundation of all creation that He will *love* His creation.

At no time does God say, "I love you whenever it's convenient. I love you when you are good. I love you as long as you agree to try harder."

Jesus said in the most famous verse of the New Testament: "For God so loved the world that he gave his one and only Son, that whoever believes in him shall not perish but have eternal life" (John 3:16). There's nothing in that statement about our earning or being worthy of God's love. All the motivation and impetus are on His part. God *so loved.* God *gave.*

When God said to mankind, "I love you," He took all that was precious to Him and most beautiful to Him, and He *gave it all up.* He said "I love you" by paying the price for our sin, and that price was the death of Jesus on the cross.

Don't ever think that genuine love is cheap. When God said to mankind, "I love you," He was saying I love you under all conditions. I love you when you are rebellious and disobedient. I love you when you turn your back on Me and refuse to love Me back. I love you when you lock Me out of your life's plan and when there is nothing in you that is deserving or worthy of My love. I love you, period, because I am Love.

THE HOLY SPIRIT REVEALS GOD'S LOVE

This awesome, unlimited, undeserved love would be unknown to us if it weren't for the witness of the Holy Spirit. We simply cannot see God's love with our own understanding. The Holy Spirit reveals that God's love was extended to us first, even when we were completely unworthy. The Holy Spirit shows us that God does not require us to clean up our sinful selves before He will love us. Rather, God sent His Son to die on our behalf when we were still in full rebellion against Him (see Romans 5:6-8).

It is the Holy Spirit who revealed to me years ago that I was owned and controlled by Satan, the evil slave master, and by a life of sin. I was living under the horrors of spiritual slavery. The Holy Spirit said to me, "I can free you! Do you want to be freed?"

At first I was reluctant to turn from my old way of life. "If I become free of this spiritual bondage," I reasoned, "I might miss out on the good things that I can get from my slave master."

Even in my spiritual blindness, the Holy Spirit graciously took me on a journey, showing me the horrors of hell, which my slave master had prepared for my eternal future. The Spirit opened my eyes to the sickness and disease that were awaiting me. He revealed to me the future pain and agony and torment that would never end. I was terrified.

Here is what the Holy Spirit told me: "Your slave master tells you he is strong and that you cannot escape his enslavement. He wants you to believe that you are too far gone to be freed and that he will always have you under his control." And then the Holy Spirit asked me, "Is that what you want?"

My answer was a resounding "No!"

Then the Spirit graciously said, "Let me introduce you to Jesus. He is much stronger than your slave master. In fact, He has already rendered Satan ineffective. Jesus *loves* you, Michael! He loves you with immeasurable, incomprehensible, unconditional love. He died for you even when you were hanging out with your slave master, and He invites you to experience all the riches that He has in store for you."

The Holy Spirit showed me through the eyes of faith what my future with this loving Savior, Jesus, would be like. He opened my eyes to the glories, joys, and blessedness of heaven. By this time I was crying from the top of my voice, "Free me!" I cried out to Jesus, "Save me from my slave master! Release me from my sin and guilt and bondage." And in His great love, He did.

God's love always motivates Him toward us with the purpose of forgiving us, restoring us, and showering His mercy and grace upon us. He doesn't wait for us to clean up our act. He pursues us because His love drives Him to seek us out. That is how much He loves us.

SIN: THE OPPOSITE OF LOVE

When I ask people to name the opposite of love, most say, "Hate." "But what is hate?" I ask. Some respond, "It's anger." Others say, "It's prejudice." Those descriptions are accurate, of course, but they fail to get at the root of the problem, which is sin. Sin causes us to tear away at people and ourselves. Sin isolates us from other people. It destroys our inner selves. Sin causes death, destruction, and loss, including estrangement from God. In other words, sin is the opposite of love.

Love, in vivid contrast, causes us to reach out to others and to build up relationships, encourage people, and promote behaviors and attitudes that create love and blessing in the lives of those around us. Love is the foremost attribute of our relationship with God—He loves us, and we love Him in response.

What is the most loving act in all history? Without a doubt it is Jesus' dying on the cross to pay the penalty for our sins. Focus your thoughts for a moment on Jesus hanging on a rough, splintery wooden cross between two criminals. What took Jesus to the undeserved shame and suffering of the cross? His love for you. For whose sake did He shed His blood? It was for your sake. For whose eternal soul did He die? He died for your soul.

Jesus hung on that cross in utter pain, anguish, and embarrassment. Roman crucifixion is the most cruel, inhuman form of execution. And Jesus suffered all of this in your place. He died so you won't have to.

And in all of this suffering, what was His greatest moment of agony? It was the moment when He took upon Himself the sins of mankind, and as a result of our sin—yours and mine—He was momentarily separated from the love of His Father. The unity between God the Father and God the Son had never been broken. Then, in one split second, it occurred. The eyes of the Father could not look upon the Son in that moment when He carried our sin upon His sinless body.

Jesus laid down His life for you that you might fully experience God's love now and forever. He did it so you might be healed and be made whole by God's love. This is the power and the limitlessness of God's love for you and for me.

THE FIRST ATTRIBUTE OF SPIRIT-LED CHARACTER

Love is at the top of the heap among the character traits identified in the Bible as the fruit of the Spirit. Bible scholars throughout the centuries have insisted that in the context of Paul's letter to the Galatians, love is not only the first trait associated with the fruit of the Spirit, but it is *synonymous* with the fruit of the Spirit. Why? Because love encompasses all the other characteristics on the list. When we demonstrate a life of biblical love, we invariably express joy, peace, patience, and so forth. Love becomes the compelling, motivating, energizing force for what we say and do.

Love, as the premier fruit of the Spirit, is not just pleasant emotions or a good feeling. It is primarily self-giving. Demonstrating biblical love is the ultimate challenge. It is the most difficult thing God calls us to do, and it is the most *potent* thing He enables us to do. In the end, the demonstration of biblical love is the most healing thing we can do for our own wounded lives, and it is the most beneficial act we can take in extending God's healing power to others.

Demonstrating love requires us to make a choice. That choice involves the way we perceive other people and the way we choose to respond to them. The choice of love is always the same choice Jesus made. It is the choice to *forgive.*

The Choice to Forgive

Love will never characterize your life if you consider other people to be your enemies or if you view them as being repulsive because they are sinners. Before you can love others, you must be able to forgive them. And to forgive them, you must be capable of seeing them as people in need of God's forgiveness. Once we see others as needing God's forgiveness, just as we need His forgiveness, then we can love them.

The story is told of a chaplain who was traveling on a train. He was seated next to a young man who was obviously agitated and anxious. The young man had just been released from prison and was on his way home to his family. He told the chaplain that his crime had brought great shame to his family name. He also mentioned that his relatives had never visited him or written to him while he was in prison. He questioned whether they still loved him.

Because he was unsure of their forgiveness, he had asked his family to give him a sign. The family property was adjacent to the railway tracks, and close to the tracks was a large apple tree. In a letter to his family, he had written: "If you forgive me and will welcome me back home, tie a white ribbon in the apple tree." If he saw a ribbon as the train passed the family property, he would get off at the next stop and return to his home. If not, he would stay on the train, travel on, and create a life apart from his family.

The closer the train came to his hometown, the more anxious the young man became. He asked the chaplain to look out the window as the train rounded a bend and came in view of the tree. The chaplain spotted the tree and put his hand on the young man's shoulder. In a quiet, broken voice, the chaplain said: "Son, there is no ribbon on the big apple tree." Before the young man could react, the chaplain continued, "There are white ribbons all over every tree, on the telephone poles, and covering the fences along the railroad track."

Much later, the chaplain gave this report: "I felt as if I had witnessed a miracle when I saw the look on this young man's face. Never had I seen a clearer picture of a person who knew without a doubt that he was loved and forgiven."

The expression of God's unconditional love *always* produces a miracle. It heals the person who experiences God's remarkable love. And it heals the person who is blessed to introduce another to God's love and forgiveness.

God's love surging in us and through us puts "white ribbons" all over our lives so that others are drawn to us in their hurt, their sorrow, and their rejection. They want the love of God for themselves. And we not only have an opportunity to love them with the love of the Lord but to point them to the love that pours from the shed blood of Jesus.

The Choice to Respond

God's love is unconditional, but He does not force us to accept it. His love is compelling, but we must decide as an act of our will to submit to the work of the Holy Spirit in our lives. God waits for our invitation as an indication of our readiness to accept the love that He longs to shower on us.

As long as we are relying on our own strength and talent and intelligence to get us through life, we won't recognize our need for the comforting presence of God's love. But when we feel deep remorse over our sin, that's when we realize our need for the forgiving mercy of God's love. When our emotions run deep and raw, that's when we turn to God and cry out, "Holy Spirit, hold me in Your everlasting arms. Comfort me with Your forgiveness, presence, and approval."

If we have such a deep need for God's love, we must also realize that those around us know the same hurts and sorrow, and they have the same hunger for mercy and forgiveness. It is an act of our will to become a vessel of God's love to others, especially when they are showing their worst nature. Biblical love demonstrates its greatest potency in tough, testing times. God's love through us is most powerful when it's the most difficult for us to demonstrate His love to others.

Think about a young couple that has just fallen in love. They are tripping all over themselves to please each other. They are on an emotional high, eager to give to the one they love. Their giving is fueled by overwhelming emotions and also by a certain degree of lust.

But then comes that first argument, that first injury to the emotions, that first wounding of rejection or misunderstanding. What is the first response we are likely to make in our fleshly, human nature? Retaliation! After all, conventional wisdom says we have a right to fight back when we are hurt. We have a right to demand justice, to give loud voice to our complaint. It would be wrong to allow the person who wounded us to get away with such hurtful behavior.

That is the way of the world, but it is completely contradictory to true biblical spirituality. God's love says we have forfeited every right to exact vengeance or to retaliate in the face of anger, hatred, or emotional wounding. God's love says only that we now have the privilege and responsibility to show love no matter what others do to us. Remember, the fruit of the Spirit is the character of God, and Jesus loved even those who crucified Him.

Love has to be our guiding principle at all times, even in the long, arid, unfeeling times when it seems that our souls are lost in a desert. True biblical love has an opportunity to shine in the midst of a life marked by a colicky baby, piles of dirty diapers, overdue bills, sickness, work pressures, and loneliness in marriage. It is then that true self-giving love is both required and desired.

Over the decades of my pastoral ministry, a number of women have told me that their husbands are courteous and thoughtful toward them in public, but these same men are rude and selfish at home. Husbands have told me that their wives are gracious and vivacious in a crowd—just as they were when they were dating—but are moody and crabby and demanding at home.

When those we love treat us with duplicity, it generates tremendous anger. The person who witnesses repeated hypocrisy in behavior—one face shown to the public, another in private—feels cheated. And in feeling anger over this hypocrisy, the impulse of our flesh is to repay evil for evil.

In marriage, revenge born of anger can show itself as passionate opposition or as cold, detached emotion. Women tend to give their husbands the silent treatment, curtly saying, "No...nothing is wrong" when everything about their body language and expression shouts otherwise. Husbands take revenge by ignoring their wives—hiding behind a newspaper, booting up the computer, watching the sports channel, or leaving the house to play golf.

But not always. In other cases, anger erupts in hot expressions of retaliation, such as screaming, crying, name calling, threatening, or even throwing things, shoving, and hitting. Neither the cold nor the hot approach to retaliation is a manifestation of biblical love.

It is in precisely those moments when we feel stepped on, deceived, ignored, or rejected that genuine biblical love has the greatest opportunity. When we maintain our demonstration and expression of love through *all* situations and circumstances, God's presence is manifested. Again and again, God gives us opportunity to make the choice to love others with His love.

When a person cuts in front of you and takes the last parking space in the lot, even though he has a bumper sticker on the back of his car that says "God loves you and so do I"...do you respond with love, or do you get out, rip the bumper sticker from his car, and shove it down his throat? When a family member disappoints you again and again, do you continue to pursue her in love, or do you turn your back and walk away, shutting her out of your life? When a coworker makes himself look good at your expense, do you respond with love, or do you seek ways to sabotage his success? By now you must realize that I face temptations just as you do, if not even greater temptations!

Riding out the ranting and raving of a teenager, obeying a parent who refuses to let you do what you want to do, continuing to be loyal to a Christian brother or sister who has wounded you emotionally…these are manifestations of love. In fact, *anytime* we confront a situation marked by anger, bitterness, hurt, or hatred with a genuine act of self-giving love, we are demonstrating God's nature.

This is how He loves us. He listens as *we* rant and rave, as we wound His beloved children, as we lash out, as we are inconsistent in our worship of Him. Again and again, God makes the choice to love us, unconditionally and infinitely and mercifully.

True spirituality includes the power to *choose* how we will respond. To respond with love is a choice, and it is the only option God makes available to those who genuinely seek to be led by His Spirit.

"There is no way anyone can live up to this standard!" you are saying. Yes, it is an impossible standard if attempted in our own power. But showing unconditional love to others does not come from a strong desire to love or from the sheer determination to love. The power to show unconditional love in the face of all that is unloving comes only as we yield all that we are before the Lord and allow His Spirit to govern our speech and actions.

Our only determination is to empty ourselves of all selfish ambitions and all destructive desires, then come to the Holy Spirit and say, "Take this empty container of my life and fill it today with Your presence, Your power, Your strength." Then and only then can your true spirituality be manifested in loving someone else, even those who misuse you. You are not the source of the love—you are only a conduit for it. Even if you are rejected, despised, criticized, or hurt, you can be empowered to show God's love.

HOW GOD'S LOVE HEALS US

God's love binds up all our emotional, mental, and spiritual wounds. It binds up broken relationships. But how?

In any area of weakness or failure, God's love says, "You are valuable. I treasure you more than anything. Whatever is wrong in you, I can heal it."

In any area in which we feel unworthy, God's love conveys, "I made you, I redeemed you, and I want you with Me forever!"

In any area in which we feel rejected or lonely, God's love says, "I have adopted you. I want you with Me! Come talk to Me. Come be with Me."

In any area in which we feel shame over our sin, God's love says, "The moment you confessed and repented is the moment that you were forgiven. You are free of shame because of My mercy. Go and sin no more."

Love restores us to the Father. It rebuilds us from the inside out. It refashions the way we see ourselves: We are loved, not bereft of love. We are lovable because God has made us the object of His love. We are capable of loving others because God now loves others through us.

Don't allow sin to keep you from God's love. Ask for and receive His forgiveness. And as you receive love and forgiveness from God, be filled with thankfulness. Don't allow guilt and shame over sin that has already been forgiven to fragment your heart.

As you rest in God's forgiveness, don't allow sin to keep you estranged from another person. Reach out to that person with forgiveness and love. Not only will you be healed in the process, but others will find themselves in position to be healed as well. Let the healing power of God's love restore your own life, and allow God to use you to bring His healing love to others.

Six

THE HEALING POWER
OF GOD'S JOY

The Joy of the Lord Defeats Envy and Jealousy

Years ago, someone noted that the best argument for Christianity is a Christian who is joyful, certain of his faith, and complete in his character. Unfortunately, one of the strongest arguments against Christianity is a believer who is somber and joyless, self-righteous and smug, feeling complacent in his consecrated state.

The New Testament mentions joy seventy times, and Christians know joy to be a remarkable feeling. We pursue a life of joy as a personal goal. Yet as much as we value and desire it, many of us fail to connect our faith with joy. Many seem to think that Sunday morning is a time to be sour. My friend, hear this and take it to heart: True spirituality finds true expression in the *joy* of the Lord!

The story is told of a young girl who made a confession of faith, joined the church, and was so delighted at becoming a Christian that she skipped home, singing all the way. When she arrived home, her stern, "religious" grandfather rebuked her. "You ought to be ashamed of yourself!" he said. "You have just joined the church, and here you are singing and dancing on the Lord's Day."

The little girl was crushed. She walked out to the barn, climbed up on the corral fence, and reached over to pat the mule standing inside the corral. She looked into its droopy face and bleary eyes and said, "Don't cry, old mule. Life isn't so bad. I guess you just have Grandfather's brand of religion."

Another story is told of a church committee that invited a preacher to come to town to hold special meetings. The committee members gathered at the railroad station to welcome their guest. As a man stepped off the train, the head of the delegation greeted him and asked, "Are you the preacher?" The man replied, "No, my ulcer just makes me look that way."

Oliver Wendell Holmes once said, "I might have entered the ministry if certain clergymen I know had not looked and acted like undertakers."

Robert Louis Stevenson made the following entry in his diary, as if it were an extraordinary phenomenon: "I have been to church today and I am not depressed."

To be joyful, of course, we must receive God's joy from the Holy Spirit. It is not something we can manufacture on our own.

Joy Is Not Happiness

Americans seem to be devoted to happiness above all things. We endure the workweek so we can relax and enjoy the weekend. The Sunday newspaper contains a thick travel section with stories and photos about exotic destinations guaranteed to bring pleasure and happiness. And every consumer good, from shampoo to automobiles to kitchen appliances, is said to hold the key to our personal happiness.

This obsession with happiness presents a problem when we talk about the joy of the Holy Spirit. In the minds of many, joy and happiness are considered to be identical. They are not. The world may speak about joy while thinking about candy (Almond Joy), a computer game accessory (joystick), or going for an unauthorized trip in a fast car (joyride). But each of these is nothing more than a moment of temporary, and sometimes illicit, happiness.

Happiness Is Temporary

One of the main distinctions between joy and happiness is that joy is an abiding quality, while happiness is nothing more than a temporary emotion. The world has a much more accurate grasp of happiness when it refers to a Happy Meal at a fast-food restaurant or a happy hour at a bar. Any happiness associated with eating and drinking is extremely temporary!

Each time we experience a moment of happiness, we tend quickly to want *another* moment of happiness. We seek more self-gratification. The sad reality, however, is that the more we try to gratify our lusts with sex, with greed-driven purchases, with drugs or alcohol, the *shorter* the satisfaction we receive and the *greater* our drive to pursue further gratification.

Happiness is elusive in all instances except one: when you happen to get what you desire. It is rooted in external pleasure or desirable activities. Because happiness is rooted in externals, it is as fleeting as the temporary satisfaction of lust—and as we all know, our lusts are never fully satisfied. They keep popping up. The rush of positive feelings is often over before the end of the event that triggered them.

Happiness Is Exhausting

The pursuit of happiness is like trying to grab a wet bar of soap—the harder you try to hold on to it, the more it slips out of your hands. It takes *work* to maintain happiness.

Benjamin Franklin once gave a stirring speech on the guarantees of the U.S. Constitution. A heckler called out, "Aw, them words don't mean nothing at all. Where is all the happiness you say it guarantees us?"

Franklin smiled and replied, "My friend, the Constitution only guarantees the American people the right to *pursue* happiness: You have to catch it yourself."

Part of what makes the pursuit of happiness so tedious is that happiness brings with it the attendant fear that it soon will be lost. This fear fuels the urge to seek self-gratification again as quickly as possible. The spiral is an increasingly rapid one. The more we pursue happiness and try to hold on to it, the more we feel we must pursue yet more happiness.

THE TRUE NATURE OF JOY

Joy, on the other hand, comes from the inside. It is independent of circumstances and events. Real joy does not come from favorable economic conditions, being accepted by society, or owning a luxury car. Joy comes from one thing alone: a sure knowledge that you are saved through the death and the resurrection of the Lord Jesus Christ. Real joy comes only from knowing that your sins are forgiven, you are in right standing with God, He is working all things together for your eternal good, and He is preparing an eternal home for you.

Jesus said, "Remain in my love...that your joy may be complete" (John 15:10-11). As we abide in the knowledge that Jesus is our Savior and the Lord of our lives, the Holy Spirit is free to manifest the character trait of joy inside us.

THE COMPARISON TRAP

Ask yourself, "What robs me of my joy?" The answer most likely will involve the words *stress, loss,* or *envy.* At the root of these feelings is our human tendency to compare ourselves to others. As we compare ourselves to others, we feel the emotions of greed, envy, or covetousness. It is only by comparison that we feel we are less than others or have feelings of loss or deprivation.

Comparison robs us of the joy that comes when we see ourselves as a unique, beloved, one-of-a-kind person created by God for a unique, blessing-filled purpose! Show me a person who delights in the way God has made her and the purpose to which God has called her, and I'll show you a person of great joy.

On the other hand, show me a person who sees himself as less than those around him, without any feeling of being blessed, beloved, or having a meaningful purpose, and I'll show you a person who is dour and sour.

Consider the man who is happily married to a woman he values and cherishes. He is content in his job and personal life. He lives in a comfortable home. His children bring him joy, and they are doing well in school. All in all, he has a good life.

Then he receives an invitation to attend his twenty-year class reunion. He discovers that many of his former classmates are earning considerably more than he is. Others have jobs that involve travel to exotic places, and many are married to spouses who are more educated and more attractive than his wife. It appears that a number of his former classmates who did not outshine him in academic achievements have attained higher social and professional status than he has.

A sense of failure begins to eat at this man. He begins to question his self-worth and to show signs of resentment toward his wife. He also harbors a secret animosity toward his successful fellow alumni, even to the point of harboring thoughts of their humiliating failure.

Did this man suddenly begin to make less money than before? Did his wife suddenly lose her former charm and attractiveness? Did his job description or position in his company change? The *only* thing that changed over the weekend was this man's attitude. The peace and contentment he used to enjoy have become infected with a virus called envy. He began to compare himself to others, and he lost his joy.

If you want to maintain the joy of the Holy Spirit, be on guard against the sin of envy. Envy and jealousy are "works of the flesh" that wage war against the spirit (see Galatians 5:17,19-21). They are called *works* of the flesh because they are two different things. Jealousy is a passionate desire *to hold on to* something that is already yours. The Lord God is described as being "jealous" for His people—He desires to keep them in close fellowship with Himself. That is a protective feeling the Lord has regarding something that rightfully belongs to Him. On a human scale, however, jealousy can consume us to the point that we see virtually everything as a potential adversary capable of winning away something that rightfully belongs to us. An extremely jealous person experiences a great deal of anxiety as she attempts to cling tightly to everything belonging to her.

Envy, on the other hand, is a desire to possess something that rightfully belongs to others. The person or possession desired can be material in nature, or it can be a desire for a relationship or a character quality, an honor or a reward. King Ahab of Israel had everything a monarch could want except for one tiny vineyard that was adjacent to his large one. The small field belonged to a man named Naboth. Ahab sulked over his failure to own this small field until his wife, Jezebel, plotted to have Naboth killed and take the man's field by force (see 1 Kings 21:1-29).

King David, who already had several wives and could have had any virgin or widow in the land as his wife, was envious of Uriah the Hittite, one of his most loyal soldiers, because Bathsheba was his wife. He arranged to have Uriah killed in battle so he could have the object of his desire (see 2 Samuel 11:1-27).

Many people who seem to have everything that a person could desire materially or financially can envy the possessions of others. Envy is incapacitating and debilitating. Proverbs 14:30 says, "A heart at peace gives life to the body, but envy rots the bones."

The apostle Paul found the solution to bone-rotting envy. He wrote:

> I have learned to be content whatever the circumstances. I
> know what it is to be in need, and I know what it is to have
> plenty. I have learned the secret of being content in any and
> every situation, whether well fed or hungry, whether living
> in plenty or in want. (Philippians 4:11-12)

Can you say the same? Is contentment your attitude even when others seem to have a better quality of life than you have?

In the end, both envy and jealousy involve a preoccupation with what we *want* to own, control, or possess. Jealousy in the extreme can cause a person to become tight-fisted, self-centered, emotionally closed off, and rigid or cold in response to the friendly overtures of other people. Envy in the extreme can cause a person to steal, to manipulate others, to deceive, and to engage in dishonest activities in order to gain what he or she wants.

Jealousy and envy eat away at our joy. They cause us to doubt God's sufficiency and His love. We live in fear that we will not have enough of what we need in order to have our basic emotional needs met. What a widespread problem this is in our nation today!

A few years ago in a television interview, Rabbi Harold Kushner commented on the self-esteem trap. The rabbi said:

> Tomorrow morning if every woman in America wakes up feeling good about her appearance, the American economy would collapse. Whole industries are built on the notion that women are anxious that they will not be lovable unless they measure up to some standard of perfection.

Kushner concluded,

> I hope you all know that the women who are really attractive to men are not the ones who look like fashion models. It is the women who feel at peace with themselves, and who are not obsessed with hair, weight, and figure to the point that they cannot even follow a conversation.

It is when a woman compares herself to a photograph in a fashion magazine that she feels inadequate. And with that comparison comes a tremendous lack of joy! The same is true for men, perhaps in slightly different ways. A man looks at the shiny new Ferrari or Mercedes cruising down the highway, then he thinks about his rusty beater and says, "I'm not as good as that guy. I don't have as much. I'm not as valuable."

Just because someone is a Christian doesn't mean he is immune from the tendency to compare. We look at the highly regarded teacher of the adult Bible class as being more valuable than we are as a helper in the nursery. We compare ourselves with others, and in the wake of our comparison, we say good-bye to joy.

Perfectionism

One of the insidious things that comparison does is cause some people to become perfectionists. After all, perfection defies comparison: It always wins!

No matter how you attempt to spiritualize it, perfectionism can give you ulcers, headaches, even a heart attack. It can turn a beautiful countenance into a hard, tense expression. It can easily turn a pleasant person into a shrew.

The story is told of a gardener who spent untold hours making his garden appear beautiful. But one year, in spite of his careful tending, his garden produced an abundance of dandelions. He tried every method to eliminate them, all to no avail. Finally, he contacted the Department of Agriculture, asking, "What shall I try next?" The reply came, "Try getting used to them."

Sometimes the best solution for perfectionism is just that simple: Learn to live with those things that you cannot change or need not change. This certainly is not to say that a person should compromise with sin! But rather than feel anxious about whether some task is done to perfection to the point of damaging a relationship, give up the perfect ideal and pursue a deeper quality of relationship.

My friend, there's only one area of envy that is permissible before God, and that is the envy an unsaved person feels toward a saved person's salvation. There's only one comparison that is acceptable to God: "I am not saved, while all these others are enjoying that taste of eternity." Why is this comparison-based envy acceptable? Because it drives that person toward surrender to Jesus!

Pleasing Yourself, Others, or God?

We often think we are doing things to please the Lord or to please others when in fact we are striving to enhance our feelings of self-worth. Countless men and women are involved in "meaningful activities" to boost their self-esteem. Think about all the people who are quick to tell you all they are doing, all the activities and responsibilities and volunteer service that are consuming their energy. People are quick to tell you about the long hours they are putting in at work. Why? They want to come out on the positive side of the comparison game.

But nothing is worthy of our time and energy if it means that we crowd Jesus out of our lives or dismiss an opportunity to sit in His presence. When we strive to maintain our sense of self-worth through "meaningful activity," we end up compromising our time with Jesus. And no amount of striving for personal value is worth the loss we experience by not spending time with the Lord. Let me state it again: *Nothing is worthy of our time and energy if it means that we crowd out an opportunity to sit at Jesus' feet.*

EXPERIENCING THE JOY OF THE LORD

Years ago a little boy was given a priceless possession—his grandfather's pocket watch. He treasured the watch, but one day while he was playing in his father's ice-manufacturing plant, he lost the watch in the midst of the ice and sawdust. He searched for it, and his search became increasingly frantic. Finally he thought, *I must be still.* When he stopped searching and listened intently, he heard the watch ticking.

The more we try to hang on to our joy with frantic efforts and frenetic activity, the more we are likely to lose our joy. Our joy is experienced most clearly when we take time to be silent before the Lord, to allow our minds and hearts to rest in His sufficiency, and to allow the Spirit of the Lord to confirm that we are recipients of His grace and His mercy, not only today, but always.

C. S. Lewis wrote, "God designed the human machine to run on Himself. That is why it is just no good asking God to make us happy in our own way without bothering about Him."[1]

What happens when we sit quietly in the Lord's presence, meditating on Him? Before long, we find ourselves *wanting* to voice thanksgiving and praise. When we stop comparing ourselves to others and fix our eyes squarely on Jesus and the goodness and majesty and power and mercy of the Lord, we can't help but praise Him!

The fact is, we can't compare ourselves to the glory of the Lord. We are finite, and He is infinite. We are weak, and He is omnipotent—all powerful, all capable. We are uninformed and limited, and He is all wise. We are bound to this earth, and He is unlimited in time and space.

Rather than comparing, we see His glory. We find ourselves face to face with His majesty and splendor and sovereignty. When we stop striving and silently regard the awe of the Lord, then our natural response is praise. We praise Him for His victory over the Enemy. And we praise Him for His endless methods of provision for our needs.

We were created for praise. It is our greatest privilege and honor. And not only does our praise honor God, the process of praise produces joy in our hearts. Praise causes us to see the creative power of God at work. It causes us to be thankful for the many blessings of God. It causes us to bask in God's love. And in the process, praise heals us. It leaches away envy, bitterness, and resentment. We don't have to strive to stake out our own corner of God's love. His love is unlimited, so we can cease striving. There's no limit on the amount of love and provision God brings to mankind. There is no limit to the rewards He has to give. We don't need to compete for them!

THREE TRUTHS ABOUT JOY

Let me remind you of three great truths about joy in light of our praise and the work it does to heal us.

Joy Is Not an Absence of Adversity or Trials

Many people assume that joy is what we experience when there is no sadness or trouble in our lives. That is not the way genuine joy works. Joy exists in the lives of those who pursue true spirituality even in the face of troubled times. Some of the greatest moments of joy in my life have occurred in situations that seemed to be dark and ominous.

One of the greatest biblical passages related to joy is Philippians 4. At the time Paul wrote to the Philippians, he was in prison. The church in Philippi had experienced economic hardships and other forms of persecution. As is true for most people who suffer over a long period of time, these believers had become vulnerable to distrust, division, and jealousy. Yet Paul wrote to these believers, "Rejoice in the Lord always. I will say it again: Rejoice!" (Philippians 4:4). He said they were his "joy and crown" and added, "I rejoice greatly in the Lord" at their renewed expressions of concern for his welfare (see Philippians 4:1,10).

This most joyful letter from a man of great joy is a clear expression that the fruit of the Spirit is manifested most clearly in times of adversity.

Joy helps us see *beyond* our immediate circumstances as it lifts our eyes to God, who is above and beyond and greater than any problem we face. Joy shines brightest in the dark moments of testing and trials.

Joy is not an absence of pain or sorrow. Rather, joy is rooted in the sure knowledge that God is with us in our pain and sorrow and that absolutely nothing can separate us from His love (see Romans 8:38-39). God is at work in you and at work on your behalf whether you are employed or unemployed, accepted or rejected by others, criticized or praised.

Praise is the vehicle that opens our eyes to the truth about the goodness and greatness of God. Praise is how we put ourselves in position to have joy *even in the midst of* adversity. Praise is what takes our eyes off the temporary state of our troubles and focuses our attention on God's eternal presence with us.

Joy Is Not a Denial of Reality nor is it False Hope for the Future

Some people believe that joy in the midst of pain and sorrow is nothing more than a denial of the reality of a difficult situation. God's Word never requires us to deny reality; rather, we are to confront reality with faith, live above the moment, and see the future that God holds out to us.

Millions of people are intensely concerned about their future. Psychic hotlines have never been so popular, and many people won't venture from their homes without reading their horoscope. People consult fortune-tellers or those who claim to "channel" contact with the dead—primarily because they want to be sure about their own future as well as the fate of others they love.

The joy of true spirituality is not a denial of the present. Rather, it is the by-product of knowing that, regardless of our circumstances, Jesus is in control of the universe. He is the Author and Finisher of our faith. He is the Beginning and the Ending of all things. And regardless of how the future may *appear,* He has all things under His control.

Praise brings us to a conscious recognition of these truths! Praise is intended to be very specific. Our praise should cover every attribute and aspect of God's character and nature that we see revealed in Scripture. If you don't know very many of those attributes, get into the Bible and see what it teaches about God. Study the names of God and the names associated with Christ. Each name gives us insight into an aspect of God's nature. Praising God for His many attributes will lead you to this conclusion: For every temporary problem you face, God has a permanent attribute that is a solution to whatever you are confronting.

Joy Is Not Based on Having Everything Under Control

Countless people believe they will feel joy if they can just get past the current crisis, pay all their current bills, meet the current deadlines. This expectation is doomed to failure and frustration because joy is not the result of our striving. Rather, it is the result of letting go of the anxiety that is associated with striving, and instead, trusting God to do His work in us and on our behalf. Joy is found in trusting God to walk through the difficult time with us, to help us with His unlimited resources to meet all the challenges we face, and to work behind the scenes to bring about blessing. Paul had very little control over his life in prison and yet he wrote, "My God will meet all your needs according to his glorious riches in Christ Jesus" (Philippians 4:19).

And what is the link to praise? We praise God not only for who He is but for all that He has done. Praise Him for the way He has worked in you and through you, arranging some aspects of your life even before you were born. Praise God for all the ways in which you see Him at work in the Scriptures. Praise Him for what He has accomplished in others and then praise Him that He desires to accomplish the same things in you.

The more you praise God for His work in your life, the more you will understand that God is in control of all things, can meet all needs, and can solve all problems. Praise redirects our attention and our energy toward what God can do and who God is—and takes our attention away from what others are achieving and what we think we should be doing.

The joy of the Lord is the joy that He has in you as His child. It is the joy that He experiences in seeing you become more like Christ. It is the joy that He feels at your worship of Him. The joy of the Lord gives us strength and heals us. The joy of the Lord brings us to wholeness.

Many Christians seem to think that the more dreary the Christian life is, the more spiritual a person becomes. Not so! The Christian life is to be marked by joy. Anytime you find yourself feeling less than joyful, go to God. Burrow into His presence and stay there. Invite Him to do His work in you.

Praise God until you feel His joy bubbling up inside you. The closer you get to the flame of the Spirit, the more glowing and radiant you will become. The closer you get to the fountain of the Spirit, the more you will overflow with His likeness. The closer you walk with Jesus, the more like Him you will become. And in all ways the joy of the Holy Spirit *will* infuse you!

Seven

THE HEALING POWER
OF GOD'S PEACE

An Untroubled Heart Frees Us from Fear

I once heard about a couple who became so alarmed at the condition of society that they decided to find the one place on earth that promised the utmost serenity. Finally, they located the perfect place and built their dream house there. The next Christmas they sent their pastor a picture of their new home in the Falkland Islands. A few months later, however, their peaceful sanctuary had become a war zone between Great Britain and Argentina!

No place on earth is immune from natural disaster, disease, or human conflict. In the days of the prophets Jeremiah and Micah, false preachers were proclaiming a false peace, a man-made peace without God. They created a slogan, saying "Peace, peace" even in the face of dire circumstances and sin. Jeremiah said, "They dress the wound of my people as though it were not serious. 'Peace, peace,' they say" (Jeremiah 6:14).

God, however, declared that they were proclaiming peace "when there is no peace." His judgment was sure: " 'They will fall among the fallen; they will be brought down when I punish them,' says the LORD" (Jeremiah 6:14-15).

Things are no different today. There are many who assure those living lives contrary to God's Word: "Don't worry, everybody is doing this. God doesn't really care about such minor things. After all, you're not hurting anyone." They are saying, in essence, "peace, peace" when there is no peace.

And God responds, "There is no peace for the rebellious person." All sin is serious to God. Sin must never be trivialized by man-made justifications. Only God's forgiveness can bring genuine peace.

The prophet Isaiah gave this word from the Lord:

> "I have seen his ways, but I will heal him;
>
>> I will guide him and restore comfort to him,
>>
>> creating praise on the lips of the mourners in Israel.
>
> Peace, peace, to those far and near,"
>
>> says the LORD. "And I will heal them."
>
> But the wicked are like the tossing sea,
>
>> which cannot rest,
>>
>> whose waves cast up mire and mud.
>
> "There is no peace," says my God, "for the wicked."
>
>> (Isaiah 57:18-21)

Others offer a hollow solution to those who are undergoing great sorrow or pain, saying, "Don't worry, this will pass. You'll get over it." They are saying, "Peace, peace."

And God responds, "There is no peace." No pills, no amount of sleep, no amount of time alone can heal a wounded spirit. Only God's forgiveness, comfort, and mercy can heal a wounded spirit and restore genuine peace.

A PROFILE OF GOD'S PEACE

Jesus said clearly, "Peace I leave with you; my peace I give you. I do not give to you as the world gives. Do not let your hearts be troubled and do not be afraid" (John 14:27). With these words Jesus described the root causes of worry and anxiety, which for all of us are fear and a troubled heart.

A Heart That Is Not Troubled

A troubled heart is a bigger issue than being concerned about a major presentation that you have to make at work. It's a heart that is in emotional turmoil because of sin. Guilt creates anxiety and never lets a person have a good night's rest.

Sin destroys something inside us, causing shame and worry. The person who is injured by another's sinful behavior will feel deep pain and sometimes powerlessness and a deep level of anger. The result for both the sinner and the sinned-against is turmoil within and a loss of peace.

We often lose our peace due to the words or actions of an individual, but we also can grow anxious over an encounter with the general sinfulness of mankind. Through the ages, our fallen condition has resulted in a corruption of the earth and the release of pollutants, poisons, and disease. It's easy to lose our inner peace if we are suffering from an illness caused by environmental toxins.

Anxiety also arises from life issues far less serious than chronic illness. A close cousin of fear, anxiety is a preoccupation with unimportant things and a false reasoning that if those things are resolved, life will be great. Some people say, "If I only have 'x' number of dollars, I will have peace." "Once I get married, I will have peace." The truth, however, is that these accomplishments will not bring peace because each one is temporary and as difficult to maintain as it is to achieve.

There are other ways that we create and heighten the problem of anxiety. Writing in the *Chicago Tribune,* Robert Samuelson had this to say: "We Americans are addicted to anxiety. We deplore it and claim to resist it, but we actually crave it and pursue it aggressively. We over-schedule ourselves and our children, and try to cram even more activity into the day." At the conclusion of his long article, he wrote, "All the striving and comparing infuses America with vitality and at the same time creates what may be our largest national deficit—peace of mind."[1] In our striving to be the best, do the most, and achieve the highest, we sacrifice our inner peace.

Anxiety is always at hand, but the Lord gives us license to be anxious about only one thing: our salvation. And the only reason He authorizes this one area of anxiety is so we will accept Christ Jesus as our Savior! If you do not know with certainty that you will spend eternity with Jesus Christ, you have good cause to feel anxious. The good news is that you *can* receive Jesus Christ as your Savior and erase anxiety from your life. God grants genuine peace only on the basis of righteousness, which results from our having His righteousness, and that emanates from a right relationship with Him.

A Heart Free of Fear

Isaiah 43 begins, "Fear not, for I have redeemed you; I have summoned you by name; you are mine" (verse 1). The second great foe of peace is fear, which comes in many guises, including panic, dread, and worry. Getting to the core of fear that lies behind many other emotions can be like peeling layers of wallpaper off the wall in an old house. You recognize sorrow, and beneath it you find regret. You peel back regret, and you uncover self-centeredness. You peel back self-centeredness, and you find doubt. You peel back doubt, and you find fear. Fear, ultimately, is a lack of trust in God.

We struggle with a fear of failure, of sickness, of loss, of bankruptcy, or of divorce. Parents fear a bad outcome for their children, or they fear growing old. Fear is not rational. In some cases, it is a nagging fear that cannot be readily defined or diagnosed.

In some instances, fear actually brings about the thing we fear most. We fear failure, so we avoid taking the risk of trying a new approach or learning a new method. A fear of failure can cause us to become isolated. It can cause those around us to question our motives, which in turn can cause us to fear rejection. This works to produce further isolation. The fear of failure can easily produce failure.

Years ago there was a very good auto mechanic who repaired cars with greater accuracy and efficiency than most mechanics. But then came the innovation of computerized systems in cars. This man's employer wanted to send him to school to learn how to work with the new computerized systems. But the mechanic refused, saying, "I know how to fix cars. I don't need to learn this." In his heart he was afraid he couldn't understand the new technology.

The result of his fear was the loss of his job, which added a new fear: How was he going to support his family? He decided to fix cars in the driveway of his home.

Through the years he became more and more isolated, and fewer and fewer people brought him their cars. Some of his old clients stopped coming, and others bought new cars with the computerized systems that this man couldn't repair. His wife became frustrated at his lack of ability to provide, and he soon had an added fear: the fear of losing her. His fears kept him awake at night, and sleep deprivation damaged his health. This man today has many more fears than the single fear that started it all.

Fear of Death

This man is not alone. We all struggle with fear, and the ultimate fear is a fear of dying. Even Jesus' closest followers knew this fear. We see it in the midst of a storm on the Sea of Galilee and in Peter's fearful denial of the Lord in the aftermath of Jesus' arrest. In every manifestation of the fear of death, Jesus sought to assure His followers that He is stronger than death. Ultimately, He conquered death!

Every time I look into the Scriptures and find a lack of peace, I see fear. And every time I see fear in operation, I see that faith is lacking. On the other hand, when faith is present, fear is banished. Faith has the power to banish even the fear of death. Faith answers the what-if question with a great, "So…what if? God is in control of all things, including every detail and circumstance of my life and death. I can rest in that knowledge and experience peace."

Fear of Loss

Many people fear not only material or financial loss but also a loss of relationships. Some are frightened that a child will run away. They live in fear, even though their home life is a happy and loving one. They fear rejection, infidelity, or even the loss of a loved one to incapacitating disease. A number of fears related to loss are actually phantom fears. Situations do not exist to warrant fear, but a person perceives that such a situation *might* arise.

I know Christians who are haunted by a fear that they are going to lose every dollar they have invested or saved. For most, this is an imaginary fear. A man once told me that he was consumed with fear that he was going to spend his final days in a homeless shelter. After talking with him, I discovered that his assets added up to more than a million dollars. His fear was unfounded, but still it robbed his heart of peace.

Anytime we look at a potential problem and allow it to loom larger than God in our minds and spirits, we are prone to fear. The greater our fear grows, the less we are able to see God beyond our problem. The only cure for phantom fears, as well as real fear associated with real loss, is faith.

What Fear and Anxiety Do to Us

A great deal of research has documented the harmful effects of fear and chronic anxiety. Medical researchers have concluded that fear weakens a body's stamina and saps physical energy. Fear can hamper the process of healing and also lower our resistance to disease.

Mentally, fear builds a barrier in communication. Fear causes a person to see sinister motives behind even the most innocent behavior. Fear can cause emotional and nervous breakdowns, and it is at the root of many kinds of mental disorders.

Spiritually, fear can drive a person away from God.

What about the work of anxiety? The foremost manifestation of anxiety is fear that life is going to spin out of control and we will not experience enough of what we desire most—we won't be loved enough, be recognized or honored enough, or be secure enough.

Anxiety causes people to do one of two things. First, some people try harder to bring about *enough* of what they feel is lacking. The problem is that the more people strive to achieve what they believe will satisfy their drive for recognition and value, the greater their need for recognition and value becomes. The anxious person is like a hamster running on the exercise wheel in his cage—a great deal of energy and effort is exerted, but he still makes no progress.

The second outcome of anxiety is a growing doubt of God's love, including His desire to meet one's emotional needs. This avenue for anxiety leads to a fear that God's love cannot be counted upon—His approval becomes something the person believes he or she needs to earn. And that, sadly, often leads to striving and an increase in anxiety. Ultimately, anxiety is a form of atheism—it is refusing to believe that God is capable of loving us, protecting us, and providing for us.

When we allow ourselves to be filled with anxiety, we begin to count things, including relationships with certain individuals, as more important to us than our relationship with God. We begin to derive security from the acquisition, possession, and control over things (or people) rather than turning to God for our security.

Living Without Fear and Anxiety

The Lord would not have said to us time and time again, "Fear not!" if it were not possible to live free from fear and anxiety. David wrote, "I sought the LORD, and he answered me; he delivered me from all my fears" (Psalm 34:4). The prophet Isaiah echoed this when he said, "Surely God is my salvation; I will trust and not be afraid" (Isaiah 12:2). The apostle Paul wrote to Timothy, "God did not give us a spirit of timidity [fear], but a spirit of power, of love and of self-discipline" (2 Timothy 1:7).

Note that David, Isaiah, and Paul all referred to the source of our freedom from fear: God. It is faith in God—His love, His ability, His desire to work in us and on our behalf—that gives us power to defeat fear.

Several steps are involved in overcoming fear.

First, *don't deny your concerns.* Don't "stuff" the worry or pain or doubt you feel. Don't deny your heartache or the problems that keep you awake at night. Instead, take the things that cause your anxiety to Jesus! Go to God with every fear or concern that causes you to worry, doubt, or suffer sorrow.

Second, *ask God to forgive you, heal you, and fill you with His peace.* No person can have peace apart from a daily filling of the Spirit of God and a daily walking with the Spirit, which is true spirituality. It is only as we look to God that we can experience freedom from fear. The safest, calmest, quietest, most secure place on earth is in His presence. David wrote: "In the day of trouble he will keep me safe in his dwelling; he will hide me in the shelter of his tabernacle and set me high upon a rock" (Psalm 27:5). David was not referring to a building. He was referring to the Lord's own presence.

In ancient times, kings had a secret place in their palaces called the *pavilion.* If a king wanted to hide from an enemy or find quiet solitude to sort out his thoughts, he would resort to his pavilion. All hell could be breaking loose in the kingdom or in the rest of the palace, but in his pavilion a king experienced peace.

Today, many homes in the United States are being built with "safe rooms." These rooms can withstand even the fiercest tornado. Families who have gone to these rooms in times of storms report that they feel secure and protected. The rest of the house may blow away, but in a safe room they survive without harm.

Instead of denying or running away from your problem, run to the Source of the only genuine solution to your problem. In the middle of the storm, run to the place of utmost security.

Third, *put all of your focus on God.* Get your mind off your problem and onto Him. Meditate on His goodness and greatness.

All fear is essentially based upon "what if…and then what will happen to me?" Fear is self-focused. Faith is the opposite. Faith is God-centered, based upon "God is…and God is in control."

Years ago the captain of a large ship set sail from Liverpool, England, on a voyage to New York City. The captain's family was on board. Late one night, a squall arose. The storm was so fierce that the vessel was in danger of capsizing. Everything on board that wasn't nailed or lashed down was sent tumbling. The passengers were startled awake and began to panic. Many began to get dressed in anticipation that they might need to launch the ship's lifeboats.

The captain's daughter, only eight years old, awoke and cried out in fright, "What's the matter?" When she was told that the ship had encountered a great storm, she asked, "Is Father on deck?" Assured that he was, she dropped her head back onto her pillow and was soon fast asleep, even as the wind roared and the waves crashed against the ship.

The next time you lose your peace, ask, "Is my heavenly Father on deck?" The Word of God tells us He most assuredly is on deck. He is in charge of every detail of our lives, even the details of the storms that toss us about.

Faith is believing that God is the Creator and Controller of all things. Nothing is beyond the reach of His power. Faith is believing that God desires to work all things for His good plan and purpose. Faith is believing that God is true to His Word and that He fulfills His promises. Faith is believing that nothing is beyond His awareness or concern.

Faith is believing that God loves us with an immeasurable, unconditional love and that His great desire is to forgive us, live in relationship with us, and extend to us the fullness of His mercy and blessings. Faith is believing that God will enable us to stand strong in the face of all sorts of adversity without fear.

When we turn our fear to faith, God's peace begins to fill our hearts. We are able to face all of life with greater hope. When we see God, who loves us and cares for us, as being bigger and more powerful than any problem we have, we feel confidence and courage.

Activating Our Faith

Jesus' disciples encountered a man whose son had a demon that caused him to be speechless and to have seizures. The disciples were unable to cast out the demon. When Jesus arrived, the boy immediately went into convulsions. The boy's father said to Jesus, "If you can do anything, take pity on us and help us."

Jesus responded, "'If you can'?" And then he said, "Everything is possible for him who believes."

"Immediately the boy's father exclaimed, 'I do believe. Help me overcome my unbelief!'" At that, Jesus rebuked the evil spirit in the boy and he was set free (Mark 9:14-27).

Your faith is activated when you say to Jesus: "I choose to see You as bigger than my negative situation, the answer to my need, the solution to my problem. I believe—help any unbelief that remains in me to be turned into belief."

And then we need to do what God's people have done through the ages. We need to "remind God" of His goodness extended to us in times past. We need to rehearse the great stories of victory and healing and miracles—not only in the lives of people long ago, but the manifestations of

God's great power and presence in others we know or have heard about in our generation as well as in our own lives and families.

Pick up your Bible and read aloud the words of God's truth back to God, beginning with Psalms 105, 106, and 107. Then read the Gospels, especially the chapters that reveal Jesus' power to heal and deliver. Read the promises of God that run from cover to cover in the Scriptures.

God, of course, has not forgotten what He has done or who He is. In "reminding" God, we are really reminding ourselves. We are putting back into our conscious mind the truth of God's capability and power. And in doing so, faith wells up in us.

You cannot concentrate on the great and mighty works of God—our Shield, our Fortress, our Deliverer, our Sustainer, our Help in times of trouble—and continue to concentrate on your problems. The shift in focus allows faith to rise up over your fear and to reduce it to nothing.

Choose to memorize some of the promises of God. Memorize verses that speak of His majesty and sovereignty over all things. That way, anytime moments of panic cause fear to take root, you have an arsenal of weapons to use in fighting back. Speak aloud the Word of God to your own spirit and to the situation you face (see Romans 10:17). Let His words sink deep into your spirit. They will generate and build faith within you.

How God's Peace Heals Us

Researchers have concluded that "constriction" is one of the greatest causes of disease, both physical and emotional. When blood vessels constrict, blood pressure rises, blood flow decreases—resulting in less oxygen and important nutrients going to all the cells of the body. The greater the constriction, the greater the internal stress level, leading to the release of stress hormones that can deplete or overwork various glands. Constriction creates an environment in which injury is more likely and disease is more easily contracted.

Emotionally, constriction occurs when we hold everything tightly within us. Those with constricted emotions are those whose emotions tend to be shut down or closed off. Anger, hatred, bitterness, and deep emotional pain become locked inside. A person who holds these emotions deep within tends to become antisocial, resentful of others, and depressed. All of these conditions war against the healing that God wants to bring.

Faith opens up a person to "God possibilities." Faith causes a person to believe that God can do all things, that God is acting at all times for our ultimate good, that God has a way where there seems to be no way. Even though a circumstance may seem bad at present, faith causes a person to cling to God's promise that a bright future lies ahead (and even if that future is not experienced on this earth, it most assuredly will be experienced in heaven).

The more a person opens up to release his faith in God's willingness and ability to act, the more the body relaxes—even in deep muscle tissues and vital organs—and the more the emotions are freed for positive expression, sometimes tears, sometimes laughter, sometimes expression in words.

Relaxation of physical tissues allows for growth, healing, and improved function. Unconstricted emotions very often generate greater communication and bonding with other people, including genuine, pure, generous expressions of love and joy. All of these are components of wholeness, which is the product of true spirituality.

Radiant Circles of Peace

God's peace comes to us in a way that is similar to concentric circles. Peace settles deep within us, then moves beyond us to others.

Peace in Our Hearts

First, we experience the peace of God in our hearts and minds. Our emotions and our spirit are settled, at rest—regardless of the turmoil that rages around us. Peace calms our minds and brings focus. Anxiety causes thoughts and feelings to tumble together in such rapid motion that we cannot focus on what we need to do to respond to a negative situation. As our minds and hearts become calmer, we are more open to God's wisdom—a clear, rational, objective awareness of our problems emerges, and along with an understanding of what is wrong can come an understanding of how God desires to work in us and through us to resolve what is wrong.

Peaceful Behavior

A second realm of peace has to do with our outward behavior. The person who feels God's peace cannot help but act in a way that reflects the peace of God. What is inside the person manifests itself in body language, movement, expressions, language, and all forms of behavior toward others.

Those who have deep peace exercise a calming effect on those they encounter. They help bring peace to others, even to individuals or groups of people who are in conflict. Peace is not taught as much as it is "caught"—it is contagious at the deepest emotional level.

Peace Among Brethren

The greater work of peace is not from believer to unbeliever, but from believer to believer. One believer who genuinely experiences God's peace can be of tremendous help to another who is going through a difficult time. It is the peace-filled believer who is in the best position to remind others of God's faithfulness, God's promise of help, protection, and provision, and God's assurance that He is with us always. The peace-filled believer is in the best position to encourage faith in others and to inspire hope that God has a way of working all things to our eternal benefit.

A Peaceful Witness

The concentric circles of peace continue to push outward. As others in a broader community see a group of loving, faith-filled, wisdom-pursuing believers resolving their problems with the peace of God reigning in their hearts, they very often seek to align themselves with these peaceful problem solvers and to ask about the source of the peace they have in their lives. In this way a person of God's peace can impact an entire community. A peaceful person can help create a peaceful family, and a peaceful family can have a great impact in creating a peaceful neighborhood and church, and a peaceful neighborhood and church can do a great deal to generate peace in a city, in a state, and in a nation.

At every step of the way, the gospel can be shared in fertile soil. Those who are confronted with love and peace are much more likely to respond positively to Jesus. Those who see manifestations of the love, joy, and peace of God are drawn to the Lord. People want peace, and they especially want a peace that works in practical ways to bring about healing and wholeness.

Making the Choice for Peace

Like love and joy, peace is a choice we are invited to make. The Bible teaches, "Whoever would love life and see good days...must seek peace and pursue it" (1 Peter 3:10-11). Jesus said, "Do not let your hearts be troubled and do not be afraid" (John 14:27). We are capable of choosing *not* to have a troubled mind and *not* to give in to fear. We can choose to repent of sin, to receive God's forgiveness and His healing of sin's consequences. We can choose to use our faith to combat our fear; we can choose to trust God to employ His infinite power, wisdom, and love on our behalf. We can choose to believe and to build up our faith through the voicing of God's Word to our own hearts.

In choosing to have trouble-free minds and hearts, we are putting ourselves into a position for the Holy Spirit to fill our lives with His peace. Repentance and faith are what *we* do. Peace is what He gives—as Jesus said, "My peace I give you. I do not give to you as the world gives" (John 14:27).

God's peace is enduring. It encompasses all of life, extending outward from us to others. It heals us and restores us and brings us to wholeness. And we can enjoy the healing work of peace in our own lives as we extend the healing power of peace to others.

Eight

THE HEALING POWER OF GOD'S PATIENCE

The Key to Waiting on God

Not long ago I went to a large bookstore to see if I could find a book on patience. I came away empty-handed. Patience is something most people want, but it's not a popular book topic! I have a hunch why we don't see books on patience making the bestseller list: Few authors feel qualified to discuss the subject.

In this regard, authors are like the rest of us. Very few people are able to develop and then *maintain* patience.

Our society is based on getting everything *now,* with instant food and beverages, voice-activated speed dialing, home-computer publishing. We seek faster methods that will bring us even quicker results. We demand more drive-through conveniences, shorter lines, faster service. We want to lose ten pounds in three days, win a fortune overnight, and fall madly in love at first sight. Perhaps if a book were written on patience, it would fail due to the small number of people who would have the patience to read it!

Christians are not immune. We want instant answers to prayer, quick holiness, ready-made spiritual maturity, and miracles on demand.

As I write this, I admit that I'm not an expert on patience. When I know what it is that God desires to see accomplished, I roll up my sleeves, rally the troops, and see that the job gets done—*sooner,* not later. I have to remind myself that God took six months to reveal to Noah the best parking place for the ark!

A number of years ago, a minister in Southern California was running late. He was scheduled to speak at an all-day conference, but it looked as if he was going to miss the opening ceremony. In his haste to make up for lost time, he cut himself shaving. Then he discovered his shirt was not ironed, and when he went out to his car, he saw that one tire was flat. Disgusted and more than a little distraught, he finally got on his way. With a sudden burst of speed, he raced through a stop sign, and a police officer signaled for the pastor to pull over. The agitated minister jumped out of his car and spoke angrily as he thrust his driver's license toward the policeman. "Go ahead," he sputtered. "Give me a ticket. Everything else has gone wrong today!"

The policeman took the driver's license from the pastor's hand and said quietly, "Sir, I used to have days like this…before I was a Christian."

ANGER: THE ENEMY OF PATIENCE

Impatience is marked by many emotions: frustration, angst, and feelings of being frantic or out of control. At the root of impatience, however, is anger.

The Greek word for patience, *makrothumia,* is made up of two words: *anger* and *slow/long.* Half of the Greek word means "anger," which includes frustration. The other half means either "long in coming" or "slow in appearing." The combination, therefore, is a concept of patience in which anger is delayed, frustration is long in coming to a head.

God is our best example of patience. He revealed His nature to Moses, saying: "The LORD, the LORD, the compassionate and gracious God, slow to anger, abounding in love and faithfulness, maintaining love to thousands, and forgiving wickedness, rebellion and sin" (Exodus 34:6-7).

The Lord describes Himself as being *slow* to anger. We can easily see that the opposite of patience is quickness in becoming angry. When someone speaks to us rudely or cuts us off in traffic, we experience an outburst of spontaneous anger or a quick eruption of frustration. Quick anger is irrational and negative and nearly always vindictive or vengeful.

We need to be precise when we deal with the subject of anger. Too many people believe that anger in all forms is wrong, and fewer still are willing to acknowledge that anger of any kind is part of God's nature. Anger in many cases is used by God to motivate us toward righteousness. Anger is an emotion that should cause us to seek justice and combat evil. God is angry at anything and anyone who harms His children or attempts to thwart His blessings. His anger, however, is always tempered by His love. And it is His love that causes His anger to be slow in manifestation.

God's love and anger are two sides of the same coin. Because God loves humanity, He feels anger toward anyone or anything that mars His masterpiece of creation. Because of His love, He is angered at sin and the destruction it brings. Because of His love, He sent His own Son to a cross so that all who believe in Him might be spared His anger at sin.

There are people who have difficulty accepting that our God of love is also a God of anger. But those who desire a God without any anger, wrath, or justice are left with a God who is weak and lazy and can't be bothered by sin. Such a God would be ineffectual, indecisive, and bland. Such a God could not be counted on to rise up against the evil that attempts to destroy our life, our family, and our faith.

On the other hand, those who emphasize God's anger and judgment—and do not recognize His incredible, vast love—are left with a God who is bent on retribution. Such a God may be powerful, but He is not someone we desire to be close to. Believing in a God who is all justice and no mercy leaves a person feeling uneasy, striving for acceptance, and lacking confidence. If we have a clouded picture of God's character and how He functions, we will have a clouded picture of how the Holy Spirit desires to produce patience within us and manifest patience through us.

SEEKING A GODLY BALANCE

God's character is a perfect balance between love and justice—between mercy and anger toward sin. This divine balance is described in the New Testament:

> The Lord is not slow in keeping his promise, as some understand slowness. He is patient with you, not wanting anyone to perish, but everyone to come to repentance.
>
> But the day of the Lord will come like a thief. The heavens will disappear with a roar; the elements will be destroyed by fire, and the earth and everything in it will be laid bare. (2 Peter 3:9-10)

Peter wrote those words to Christians who were starting to believe that because Jesus had not returned already, He was not coming at all. Peter encouraged them to be patient: Jesus *will* keep His promise to return, and the reason He hasn't already returned to judge the world is because He is patient. He is allowing time for more people to repent of their sins and accept Him as Savior.

When the Lord does act in judgment, His judgment is swift and sure. There is no compromise. It is His patience—His slowness in coming to this point of final justice—that gives men and women an opportunity to seek His mercy, love, and forgiveness.

Slowness to Anger

In His love and mercy, God patiently waits for us to respond to His invitation. He isn't denying His anger toward sin and evil, but He is lovingly waiting for us to seek His forgiveness. We are not nearly so patient. I am amused by people who say, "I am *not* angry about this situation!" My response is usually, "If you aren't angry, then why do you need to bring up the matter?"

Far better than denying your anger, you need to acknowledge it. Rather than seething in silence, it is better to say, "I am angry right now!" And even if you don't feel you can discuss it immediately, you can always say, "As soon as I cool off, I want to talk about this with you. I will tell you why I am angry and what I think needs to be done. Then we can work together toward a solution."

We commonly rely on one of two ineffective responses to anger: a spontaneous expression of angry feelings or a denial and suppression of those feelings. Neither of these is health producing.

The Spontaneous Expression of Anger

Anger that is spontaneously expressed is often far out of proportion to the circumstance that triggered it. People often justify such an outburst with the rationale that "I'm just being honest about the way I feel." In truth, however, the person is not being honest with herself when it comes to the damage that her outbursts cause—both to herself and to the person who is the recipient of her angry words. Hot anger does not reflect the character of God. Instead, it is a blatant expression of pride. It is an arrogant demand that "things be done my way, or you will pay."

This type of hot, spontaneously expressed anger causes blood pressure to rise and harmful stress hormones to be released into the bloodstream. It increases tension between people. It destroys tender feelings of compassion. It inflicts a deadly blow against creativity, opportunities for ministry, and expressions of care. There is nothing healthful—either physically or emotionally—about hot anger. It is the prideful venting of negative emotions without eliminating any of the negativity associated with those emotions.

Suppression and Denial of Anger

The opposite response—which is equally unhealthy—is to suppress feelings of anger. This anger is stone-faced in its silence. Those who suppress anger mistakenly believe that any expression of anger is unspiritual. Suppressed anger doesn't disappear, however. It just goes underground where it can fester and one day erupt like a volcano. Meanwhile, it manifests itself in an attitude of cold fury and bitter resentment. Holding anger inside brings a hardness of heart and very little flexibility or forgiveness toward other people.

When anger is turned inward, it does great damage to a person's emotions and physical health. True spirituality can lead both suppressors and hotheads to the best way to express anger positively and to allow the patience of God's Spirit to bring healing to their lives.

THE EXAMPLE SET BY JESUS

One of the most vivid demonstrations of godly anger is that of Jesus' cleansing the temple. The gospel of Matthew tells us:

> Jesus entered the temple area and drove out all who were
> buying and selling there. He overturned the tables of the
> money changers and the benches of those selling doves. "It
> is written," he said to them, "'My house will be called a
> house of prayer,' but you are making it a 'den of robbers.'"
> (21:12-13)

If slowness to anger is a mark of God's patience, then how does Jesus' eruption in the temple demonstrate patience? First, remember that Jesus had been in the temple many times. He had taught there, performed miracles there, and worshiped there. The event that Matthew describes took place during the last week of Jesus' life on earth. He had given the temple authorities all the time He had available to clean their own house. He had been extremely patient with them.

Second, recognize that Jesus did no harm to any person in the temple, and there is no evidence that any person suffered any material loss. He overturned the tables of the money changers and the stalls in which doves were being sold, but there's no mention that any money or other property was lost. Jesus was simply removing this aspect of buying sacrifices from the temple itself. He was cleansing the temple so it might be reserved for its God-intended purpose: worship in service, the preaching of God's truth.

Third, notice that Jesus' anger did not linger. The very next verse in this passage states, "The blind and the lame came to him at the temple, and he healed them" (Matthew 21:14). Jesus was able to lay aside any emotion associated with His overturning of the commercialism in the temple and move immediately into ministry. Only the chief priests and other religious authorities held on to their anger, seeing Jesus' action as an assault on their power base.

Jesus' actions in the temple were long in coming. They were carried out according to God's timing. They were definitive, and they accomplished their godly goal. Nobody was injured, and no property was destroyed. Ministry continued immediately afterward. What a useful model for us to follow in all actions that might fall under the banner of righteous indignation.

Major Causes of Impatience

Our impatience and our spontaneous expressions of anger are drawn from a deep well, and it is impossible to address all the causes. For now, let's examine five of the most common occasions for impatience.

A Narrow Worldview

Sometimes a person's horizon becomes too narrow, and he focuses only on his own needs and his own little world. That person then becomes impatient when his needs go unmet, when his schedule is interrupted, or when his opinions are challenged. Anytime a person loses sight of God's big picture—God's ultimate plan and purpose for humanity and the moving of His Spirit—he is in danger of become easily angered at every minor crisis.

One of the reasons that children are often impatient and demanding is that they have no sense of the big picture. They can't fathom consequences or situations that are likely to occur down the road. They believe the world revolves around them. They are self-focused.

The story is told of a father and son who were driving from New Mexico to Colorado on a fishing trip. The son asked, "How many more miles till we get there?" The father said, "Two hundred fifty." A while later the boy asked, "How many more miles will it be?" The father said, "One hundred fifty." Less than an hour later, the boy asked again, "How many more miles?" The father answered, "One hundred."

Finally the boy asked, "Will we get there before my sixth birthday?"

This boy was lacking the perspective of time. When we get a view of the long run, and especially catch a glimpse into the infinity of eternity, many things come into perspective. This is the eternal perspective we need to battle anger and cultivate patience. The more a person loses sight of her eternal home in heaven, the more impatient she becomes with the aggravations of life. The more a person is focused on meeting her own needs, the more impatient she becomes with the needs of others. The more a person loses sight of the forgiveness that God extends to sinners, the more he becomes impatient with those who sin against him.

Have you focused your attention on your needs and desires? If so, ask God to enlarge your view to see beyond today, beyond yourself, and beyond your immediate sphere of work and home. When you become aggravated, ask yourself: "What is this inconvenience or this insult in comparison to the glory of eternity with Christ Jesus in heaven?"

A Need for Visible Evidence

A second major cause of anger is the need for concrete, visible *evidence* that things are improving. We forget that God is *always* at work on our behalf, even when we do not sense that things are turning away from evil or are moving in a godly direction. True spirituality produces patience that stems from a deep certainty that the person who has accepted Jesus Christ as Savior will *never* be forsaken. True spirituality produces patience that springs from the expectancy that God loves His children and cares for every detail of their lives.

Farmers seem to understand patience in a way that many others do not. A farmer does not keep digging up a seed to make sure it is germinating. The person who does this will never reap a harvest. A farmer understands that various crops have different growing seasons and different lengths of time for producing fruit. A farmer doesn't confuse waiting with laziness—he continues to cultivate the soil, irrigate and fertilize the plants, and prepare his equipment and barns for the coming harvest.

Unrealistic Expectations of Others

A third major cause of impatience is the expectation of an unrealistic outcome.

The story is told of a mother who was walking in a crowded mall with her little girl. Her daughter kept tugging on her skirt, refused to cooperate, and kept up a near-constant whine of complaint. Finally, the annoyed mother began pleading, "Quiet, Cynthia. Be patient, Cynthia. Calm down, Cynthia."

A shopkeeper looked at the distraught mother and said, "I see your daughter's name is Cynthia."

The mother replied, "No, her name is Amy. *I'm* Cynthia."

Don't expect too much of those who are younger, less experienced, less talented, or less mature in their faith. Rather, exert extra patience as you help them, bless them, and encourage them. Too often we expect others to function just as we do, and then we are disappointed that they don't. There are likely others who are expecting us to function as *they* do and are disappointed when we don't! We need to develop realistic expectations of one another.

Unrealistic Expectations of Time

A fourth source of impatience is the unrealistic expectation of the passage of time. As you read this humorous spin on Psalm 23, think about your own tendency to hurry:

> The clock is my dictator. I shall not rest.
> It makes me lie down only when exhausted.
> It leads me to deep depression.
> It hounds my soul.
> It leads me in the circle of frenzy for activity's sake.
> Even though I run frantically from task to task, I will never
> get it all done. For my "ideal" is with me.
> Deadlines and my need for approval, they drain me.
> They demand performance from me beyond the limits of
> my schedule. They anoint my head with migraines.
> My in-basket overflows.
> Surely fatigue and time pressure shall follow me all the days
> of my life. And I will dwell in the bonds of my
> frustrations forever.[1]

I don't include this to indicate that we should not accomplish as much as possible in a day. God expects us to be faithful, wise, and diligent in the use of all our resources. But anxiety sets in when we believe that *we* are responsible for the results of our work, or when we come to believe that our work can earn us more of God's favor. Neither is true.

Our best efforts sometimes come to naught. Our greatest giving sometimes goes unappreciated. Nothing about our efforts or accomplishments can cause God to love us more or value us more highly.

Out-of-Balance Priorities

Our society is out of balance. Drivers speed through yellow traffic lights to save a few seconds so they can wait for hours to tee off at their favorite golf course. Businessmen gulp down coffee and frantically drive to the lake so they can sit in a small boat for hours hoping to catch a fish. People race through appointments so they can get home a little sooner so they can sit in front of the television.

When we allow our priorities to get out of balance, we will always find ourselves becoming frustrated and impatient. We must set ourselves to placing God first, our families second, and all other concerns third. When we are living according to God's guidance and within His perfect plan, the urgency of lesser matters takes a backseat.

RECOGNIZING FALSE PATIENCE

As we study the spiritual fruit of patience, we need to recognize three traits that often are confused with patience. These imposters are what I call "fake endurance."

A Lack of Compassion or Empathy

Some people can spot injustice and then just walk by it as if they don't see it. They have no empathy for those who have legitimate needs. They have no compassion for those who are spiritually lost, emotionally or mentally ill, or materially impoverished. They give the impression of being calm and patient, when in truth they are too self-absorbed to be aware of their own blindness and hardness.

Pride

There are those who feel anger at a situation, but they refuse to exert themselves to confront the evil because they fear their involvement will cause them to lose face. They are too proud to get involved, although they may rationalize their inaction with "live and let live" or "I'm not an authority on this."

Don't let false patience become an easy excuse. Certain situations cry out for justice. They are so evil that they demand a response. We must never be too self-absorbed or too complacent that we don't become angry enough to take action against all forms of evil and injustice toward God's innocent ones and beloved saints.

Grit-Your-Teeth Patience

A third form of fake endurance is not a sin, but neither is it the spiritual fruit of patience. Instead, it is human-generated patience. This is the patience that a person exhibits totally from self-motivation: "I will not lose my temper, I will not overreact, I will not let this bother me." The person usually has his hands clenched so tightly the circulation is about to be cut off, and his teeth clenched so tightly he's in danger of locking his jaw. Such patience doesn't last long and has great potential for erupting in hot anger or turning inward to suppressed anger. It is a temporary, human fix for anger that will resurface later in a more explosive form.

SPIRIT-PRODUCED PATIENCE

The only source of genuine long-suffering and patience is the Holy Spirit of God. We glorify God when we are long-suffering toward those who persecute us for taking a stand for Christ Jesus, when we are long-suffering in our loving actions to confront sin and evil, when we are patient but steadfast in our refusal to give in to temptation. It is then that we are demonstrating the fruit of the Spirit.

When we don't see an immediate turnaround from evil to good or don't see swift justice, yet we persevere in standing up for God's righteousness, we are demonstrating the fruit of the Spirit. When we find appropriate positive outlets for our anger at sin and injustice and refuse both to suppress our anger and to erupt in anger, we are demonstrating the fruit of the Spirit. When everyone around us is taking shortcuts, and we choose instead to speak out in truth and do the right thing, we are manifesting the fruit of the Spirit.

There is no way a human can generate this kind of long-suffering patience apart from the Spirit of God, which is why God-given patience is a core aspect of true spirituality. It is not within man's capacity to be this patient in situation after situation, to the end that patience becomes a quality of character in your life. It is when the Spirit of God is pouring patience into your heart and through you to others that patience becomes something you *are*, not simply something you *do*.

The patient person is willing to continue in faith until God accomplishes His will. The patient believer stands alongside a person in need until his or her need is met. In such ways, the patient person manifests to others God's patience toward us all.

How many times has God remained closer than a heartbeat to you when you were throwing a tantrum, railing at Him for His seeming lack of concern, accusing Him of being unfair, ignoring Him because He didn't do things your way or didn't answer your prayers as soon as you made the request? My friend, He has been patient with you—and with me and with every other believer—more times than we know! He desires to kindle His patience in our hearts and to demonstrate it to others through us.

POSITIONING OURSELVES FOR GOD'S PATIENCE

How do we put ourselves into the best possible position to be filled with God's patience? There are several things we can do.

Recognize the Enemy

Satan is the single source of our impatience. If he can find a way to sap your strength in the small skirmishes of life, he rarely will have to fight a big battle with you. He'll have you so tied up in knots over the small stuff that you'll never get around to taking him on in the big issues related to evil. If Satan can entangle you in mixed-up priorities, false expectations regarding people and time, or a narrow worldview, then he will have you in a trap. If he can wrap you up with a preoccupation about your own needs, your schedule, your ambitions, he will have succeeded in drawing you away from reliance upon the Holy Spirit. Recognize these schemes and face the Enemy of your soul squarely.

Pause or Slow Down

Once you have recognized the Enemy, stop the carousel of your life for a while. Step back and look at your life. Pause for reflection. It's precisely when you feel yourself overwhelmed by so much to do that you *most* need to take a break. Jesus frequently retreated from the crowds, and even His disciples, to spend time alone with the Lord. We should never feel guilty for setting aside time just to rest in the Lord's presence or to seek His face. Only when we become still before Him do we clearly hear His voice.

Ask God to Help You

As you confront the Enemy and set aside time to be with the Lord, ask God to help you see the big picture of His plan and His eternal purposes. Ask Him to help you line up your priorities and your schedule with His goals for you. In so many cases, it is not what you do right this minute that counts most, but what you do consistently over time. And in all cases, it is not what is done for your pleasure that counts, but what you do for Christ that will last through eternity.

How God's Patience Heals Us

Godly patience puts us in a position where we are both willing and empowered to do things on God's timetable, based on His deadlines. If God has made known to you a task, a calling, or a certain ministry, then immediately do what God requires of you. If you think you don't have the time, then consider the demands that originate with you or with those around you. Those things, in the majority of cases, do not require your immediate attention.

A woman once complained to me that her husband never appreciated the things she did around the house and never helped with their children. I asked her for an example.

She said, "Just yesterday I spent two hours waxing the kitchen floor.

It looked great, but the kids and the dog came barreling through, and in an instant all my work was ruined. The wax hadn't set, so everything was smeared, plus the wax on their shoes was tracked onto the dining room carpet. I got upset at the children and sent them to their rooms.

"Then my husband came home and asked how my day had gone. I told him what had happened and asked him to discipline the children, but he refused. He seemed to blame *me* for not telling the children to avoid using the back door. He didn't seem to care one way or the other if the floor was *ever* waxed."

In telling her story, the woman got even more upset. Not only was she demonstrating a lack of peace and joy, but she was very impatient with those she loved the most.

I asked her, "Did God ask you to wax the floor?"

"No," she said.

"Well, if God didn't ask you to wax the floor, and your husband doesn't care if the floor is waxed, who wanted it to be done?"

"I did," she said.

"Do you like waxing floors?" I asked with a smile.

She seemed to relax. "No. I *hate* waxing the floor." And then she said, "I guess I do it because my mother told me it was important."

I asked her, "Is a waxed floor worth losing patience with your children and your husband?"

"No," she said, almost in a whisper. "It's not worth it."

We prayed together, and I asked her to ask God what He wanted her to do. I suggested she ask God every morning, "What do You want me to do today?"

I saw this woman a week later and asked, "How did your week go?"

She said, "I went to the park three times with my children, and on one of those outings my husband joined us for a picnic. I spent more time in prayer and reading my Bible this week. I visited a friend in the hospital." Then she smiled and said, "I didn't even *think* about waxing the kitchen floor."

Her patience had been restored not because she had willed patience into her life, but because she had slowed down and asked God to fill her with His patience and to help her see what is truly important in life. When we do this, we find the rhythm of activity and the level of exertion that God desires for us, for the purposes God has for us, on the timetable God has set for us. That is what true spirituality is all about.

When we manifest the patience of the Holy Spirit, we become a true partner in the process of God's revealing Himself to us and to others through us. And in this process, we will find that God is healing our life.

Nine

THE HEALING POWER
OF GOD'S KINDNESS

The Divine Antidote to Selfishness

More and more, America's advertising industry appeals to the worst in human nature to sell us things. Hardly a product is marketed without an appeal to selfishness and self-interest. We are told: "It may be expensive, but you *deserve* it." We are worthy of this cure for baldness, that expensive perfume, this luxury automobile. In other words, we deserve to live in a pain-free, odor-free, carefree world. Need is never the issue. What we *want* is the issue.

It's no mystery why this sales pitch is so effective. Many of us have never moved beyond the obstinate cry of a two-year-old: "I want, I want, I want." Selfishness is not a fringe issue, but the very heart of pride. For a person to be genuinely selfish, he has to believe he has the *right* to be selfish. This is how selfishness becomes a good thing in our culture. The selfish person believes she has a right to look out for herself and to secure the best for herself—even at the expense of others. No price is too high to pay when pursuing one exhilarating experience after another.

While selfishness appeals to our hunger for ease and pleasure, it poisons our spirit by choking out the fruit of kindness. Selfishness cannot coexist with kindness: One will prevail and stamp out the other. In fact, selfishness perverts the concept of kindness.

PERVERTED VIRTUES

We live in a world in which people fight vigorously to preserve the right to kill a baby in the womb—the furthest thing from an act of kindness to that child. Those who fight for this right are often the very ones who are militant animal rights activists, citing kindness as a good reason to preserve the life of any animal that seems to be in jeopardy—be it a stray dog, a species that is endangered in the wild, or a laboratory rat. Our kindness is often directed at just about all God's creatures *except* our fellow man.

Others err when they mistake kindness for weakness. They see it as evidence that we are not willing to stand up for our rights. They equate kindness with a doormat mentality.

Lady Macbeth voiced these complaints about her husband, whom she feared was too full of the milk of human kindness. To Lady Macbeth, there was nothing as inconvenient as taking time to be kind to those whom she felt she would be better off without. In her view, people were to be used.

Even for those who rank higher on the kindness scale than Shakespeare's cold-hearted Lady Macbeth, too many people today see kindness as a "nice option" rather than as an essential reflection of the character of God. People are kind if it's convenient, if they happen to be in the right mood, or if showing kindness can serve their own purposes. This is not the kindness of the Holy Spirit!

The kindness we read about in the Bible is a basic *necessity;* it is part and parcel of true spirituality. It is not considered out of fashion, and it's definitely not a matter of personal convenience. It is a vital characteristic for our spirituality because it is a vital characteristic of God's own nature.

God's revelation of Himself to mankind is based on His kindness. It was out of kindness that God made a covenant with Israel, and out of kindness that He kept His side of the covenant despite the rebellion and blatant disobedience of His people. It was out of kindness that God left the splendor and majesty of heaven and became a man. Out of kindness, God chose to hang on a criminal's cross to pay the wages of sin for all who might believe in Him. It is out of kindness that God accepts repentant sinners and provides for us what we do not deserve to have.

In a world where shadow spirituality regards self-promotion as a virtue, true spirituality calls us to bear the fruit of kindness. Kindness is an expression of generosity toward others. It is a turning of self "inside out" to give to others, not only of our material resources, but of our time, presence, good wishes, and affection.

Kindness is grown in the human heart by the Holy Spirit of God. It is entirely the work of the Spirit and not generated from our own goodness. Kindness occurs as a by-product of our being filled daily with the Spirit of God and seeking to manifest His life in the world.

In 1940 researchers studied forty-three American cities and concluded that Rochester, New York, was the kindest city in the United States. A little more than fifty years later, the study was repeated in the same cities, and again Rochester was determined to be the kindest city. The researchers used an elaborate procedure by which they came to this conclusion. One writer determined to find out why Rochester came out on top. His own research led him to conclude that the city's history of kindness and generosity stemmed from its earliest days.

In the mid-1800s, renowned evangelist Charles Finney spent six months preaching the gospel and conducting prayer meetings in Rochester. Thousands upon thousands were converted to Christ. One of the marks of this particular Holy Spirit revival was that new believers renounced their selfishness and began to give of themselves to others. For a century and a half, the city had maintained a strong track record of generosity and kindness.[1]

Indeed, the Holy Spirit is the author of *all* genuine kindness. When people speak of "random acts of kindness," they are mistaken. There is nothing random about the manifestation of God's kindness in us and through us. Acts of kindness are not intended to be performed on a whim. We are to be kind *at all times, in all places, to all people.* That is the way the Holy Spirit shows His kindness to us!

The New Age philosophers of shadow spirituality teach their followers to do acts of kindness in order to feel good about themselves. Kindness is regarded as a feel-good activity, something that gives rise to our own self-esteem.

In sharp contrast, the true spirituality of God's Holy Spirit calls us to take no thought for ourselves but to seek the good of others. We are not to be motivated by the reward that doing a good deed may bring our way, but rather by what a good deed might do to help another person or to encourage another person to draw closer to Christ.

THE MARKS OF GOD'S KINDNESS

Kindness is not a hit-or-miss process of doing nice things. It is characterized by traits that are clearly defined in the Bible.

Empathy

First, the person who manifests Spirit-endued kindness has an ability to empathize with others by putting herself in another's place. So many people find it easy to forget what they experienced when they were children or teenagers; the kind person has a way of remembering. Others find it difficult to remember times of failure or weakness. Rigidity and lack of sympathy are by-products of forgetting our own shortcomings, past needs, failures, weaknesses, and indebtedness to others. Kindness involves an ability to *remember* the people we once were and to reach out to others to help them become the people they might one day become.

Kindness calls us to reach out to the person who is in bondage to sin and to speak words that bring about repentance and forgiveness. Kindness calls us to remember that we, too, were once sinners in need of a Savior.

Mercy to Self

Second, the person who manifests Spirit-endued kindness is one who can also show kindness to himself. This kindness is not self-indulgent, but rather merciful. Earlier I said that we cannot forgive ourselves; we only receive God's forgiveness. The kind person is able to let go of her past failure and sin and say, "I have been forgiven by God. I will not beat myself up over sin that God has already forgiven." The kind person not only remembers that he was once a sinner, but he also remembers that he is now saved and is declared a joint heir of all the riches of Christ's eternal glory.

What would it have been like if the apostle Paul had allowed his former life—including his murderous persecution of Christians—to dominate his thinking? What if he had felt so unworthy of God's forgiveness that he never spoke to anyone about Christ Jesus? He certainly never would have accomplished for God what he did accomplish!

Instead of taking on the role of punisher for his own past and forgiven sins, Paul said, "Forgetting what is behind and straining toward what is ahead, I press on toward the goal" of pursuing Christ and of being Christ's witness wherever and whenever he found opportunity (Philippians 3:13-14).

Receiving Kindness

Third, the person who manifests Spirit-endued kindness is one who is able to receive the kind expressions of others.

For a number of years this was an area in which I really struggled. I found it easy to show kindness, but difficult to *accept* kindness. Then a dear friend and mentor said to me, "When you refuse to accept the kindness of others, you are depriving them of the joy of showing kindness." It took a long time for this truth to sink in. Now I find myself more and more willing to receive the kindness of others because this means I am giving them an opportunity to experience more of God's joy and fulfillment in their own lives!

Letting Go of Hatred

Fourth, the person who manifests Spirit-endued kindness must be willing to let go of hatred, bitterness, and resentment. A person cannot manifest genuine kindness and allow an imaginary war to be fought in her mind.

Imaginary wars occur when you muse over disagreements that you have had with your spouse or coworker or friend. The more you harbor he-said-I-said and she-did-I-did scenarios, the more you fuel feelings of anger, hatred, and bitterness. As you harbor these imaginary wars, a relationship deteriorates to the point where you will find it virtually impossible to express a kind word or make a kind gesture to the other person.

The story is told of a man who had a flat tire on a dark, lonely road. He didn't have a jack in his car, but as he peered into the darkness, he saw a light coming from a house in the distance. He decided to walk to the house to ask if he could borrow a jack.

As he walked he carried on an imaginary conversation in his mind. What if the person who answered the door was rude and hateful or came to the door with a shotgun in his hand? What if the homeowner was so angry about being disturbed that she lashed out in anger?

The closer this man got to the house, the more his imaginary war escalated. By the time he knocked on the door, his mind was reeling. He yelled at the man as he opened the door, "I don't need your stupid jack!"

We actually sabotage our own welfare when we harbor a lack of kindness. Bitterness and resentment produce nothing good in our own lives, and they prevent us from doing good to others. When we blow a situation out of proportion, it fuels feelings of bitterness, resentment, and hatred. We start "fighting" for self, feeling that something of our dignity is about to be taken from us. Nine times out of ten, the other person involved doesn't even know he's in a war!

To put an end to this needless war, we need to exercise God's kindness. Kindness becomes the tenor of our heart as we show kindness to others. The feelings do not come first; they flow from the actions we take in reaching out to others. And as is true of the other traits of spiritual character, the more we show kindness to others, the more often we find opportunities for expressing kindness.

WHAT KINDNESS REQUIRES OF US

Many people consider kindness to be time consuming and demanding, an invasion of their privacy. They are correct! Kindness cuts short our plans and our self-indulgence. Kindness requires something from us. Specifically, it requires our risking rejection, giving time, and giving treasure.

Risking Rejection

When we extend kindness to another, there is no guarantee that the person will respond in kind. He might resist our kindness and reject us in the process.

A distinguished judge once said, "I have seen hundreds of juvenile offenders and their parents in my court, but never once have I seen one parent touch a youngster or put their arms around his shoulders or show physical signs of affection."

It's almost beyond me to understand how some parents can go through life without hugging or holding or kissing their children. I can only conclude that these parents either do not know that a child needs affection or they are unwilling to risk rejection from a troublesome child.

Risking rejection is perhaps the main reason people do not step forward and show kindness to others. They will avoid saying anything to a person they can see is headed for trouble through bad choices, not wanting to risk the loss of that person's friendship. They will see someone who is struggling and will hesitate before getting involved. They are fearful that the person will rebuff their offer of help. Kindness requires that we swallow our fear of rejection and take the risk of doing what is right.

Certainly the father in the story of the prodigal son was a man willing to risk rejection. This father had already been rejected once. His younger son had demanded his portion of his inheritance even before the father died, which was a major insult in that culture. He had abandoned the family and gone into an area considered "unclean" by the Jews, where he had participated in all sorts of "unclean" activities.

Even so, Jesus said that when this younger son finally returned to his father, the father *ran* to meet him and fell on his neck, kissing him and hugging him. He was willing to risk rejection *again* to show kindness to his wayward son (see Luke 15:11-24).

Giving Time

It takes time to write a note, make a call, or stop for an encouraging conversation. It takes time to get involved in ministry that blesses others. It takes time to feed the homeless or practice a choir number. It takes time to listen to a hurting friend, console a distraught child, or comfort a grieving heart. It takes time to visit the hospital or the prison. It takes time to pray in intercession for others. In countless ways, kindness demands the giving of our time.

Giving Treasure

God's Spirit will always compel us to act in kindness by giving some of what we have to others who are in need. Kindness compels us to *want* to give to those things that God honors so that others might hear about Jesus and come to know Him as their Savior. What we give may be money. It may be blankets or clothes or bandages or sandbags or food or shelter. God has blessed us, and He calls upon us to use what He has given us to show kindness to others.

Early in the nineteenth century, King Frederick William III of Prussia found himself in a great deal of trouble. His nation was involved in a very expensive war. This occurred at the same time he was endeavoring to transform his kingdom into a modern state. He did not have the money to improve the lot of his people and fight off the nation's enemies at the same time.

After much deliberation, the king approached the women of Prussia and asked them if they would sacrifice their gold and silver jewelry so it might be melted down and turned into currency for the purchase of the things necessary for modernizing the nation and defending it. He declared that he would give each woman who gave of her gold and silver ornaments a decoration made of much less expensive bronze or iron as a token of his gratitude. On the decoration, which was in the shape of a cross, these words were inscribed: "I gave gold for iron, 1813."

The response was overwhelming! Prussian women gave of their jewelry in great quantity, and in the end, the women prized the decoration they received from the king more than they had valued their expensive gems. The bronze and iron decoration pins were a mark of sacrifice made for their nation and a mark of honor for their king. It became more fashionable in Prussia for a person to wear an iron cross than to wear gold or silver. Very quickly, the Order of the Iron Cross was established. Generosity and sacrifice for the king became a way of life, a mark of true citizenship, and a badge of honor.

Today, shadow spirituality advocates all kinds of motives for giving—none of them consistent with God's true spirituality. Some people give because it makes them feel good. Others give out of habit. Still others give out of self-serving motives.

Some years ago Miami's Flagler Street was lined with beautiful royal palm trees. Then one night vandals cut down six of these magnificent trees, and the city did not have enough money to replace them. A donor, however, soon stepped forward.

The trees that had been cut down had been about fifteen feet tall. They formed a beautiful foreground for a large Delta Airlines billboard. The new trees so generously given were thirty-five feet tall, and they completely blocked motorists' view of the Delta Airlines billboard. The donor of these trees? Eastern Airlines!

That is *not* the kind of generosity that flows out of true spirituality.

How God's Kindness Heals Us

Jesus told a story that embodies many principles about kindness:

> A man was going down from Jerusalem to Jericho, when he
> fell into the hands of robbers. They stripped him of his
> clothes, beat him and went away, leaving him half dead. A
> priest happened to be going down the same road, and when
> he saw the man, he passed by on the other side. So too, a
> Levite, when he came to the place and saw him, passed by on
> the other side. But a Samaritan, as he traveled, came where
> the man was; and when he saw him, he took pity on him.
> He went to him and bandaged his wounds, pouring on oil
> and wine. Then he put the man on his own donkey, took
> him to an inn and took care of him. The next day he took
> out two silver coins and gave them to the innkeeper. "Look
> after him," he said, "and when I return, I will reimburse you
> for any extra expense you may have." (Luke 10:30-35)

As He finished His story, Jesus asked those around him, "Which of these three do you think was a neighbor to the man who fell into the hands of robbers?" One replied, "The one who had mercy on him." Jesus' response was, "Go and do likewise" (Luke 10:36-37).

The good Samaritan was intentional in showing kindness to this Jewish man. He had empathy for him, was moved with compassion toward him, and was willing to risk rejection and even danger in ministering to his wounds. He willingly gave of his time and his resources—not just once, but as a commitment that lasted until the injured man was restored to health.

Who was healed in this particular story? Certainly the man who had fallen victim to robbers. But by extending this kindness, the Samaritan broke down certain barriers of prejudice. Samaritans and Jews didn't get along. Jesus was showing in His parable that kindness across racial and ethnic boundaries can heal the hatred, bitterness, and resentment that build up and eat away at entire groups of people.

How does God's kindness heal us? You cannot show kindness to a person and continue to hate that person. You cannot pray for a person, believing that God will act kindly on his behalf, and continue to resent the person. You cannot extend yourself in giving to a person and continue to ridicule or feel bitterness toward that person.

But kindness doesn't stop at healing relationships. It also has clear health benefits. Hatred, bitterness, and resentment create unease that eats away at the soul. Countless diseases—both physical and emotional—have been associated with bitterness.

God's Word says clearly, "Get rid of all bitterness, rage and anger, brawling and slander, along with every form of malice. Be kind and compassionate to one another, forgiving each other, just as in Christ God forgave you" (Ephesians 4:31-32).

Kindness restores the soul. It banishes hatred and gives room for love to take root. It opens your soul to the balm of Christ's healing presence. Set aside your own agenda and your fear of rejection and exercise the kindness of the Holy Spirit. You will bring healing to others and will be healed yourself in the process.

Ten

THE HEALING POWER
OF GOD'S GOODNESS

The Force That Overcomes Evil

Talk to any group of parents or teachers of young children, and you're bound to hear someone mention attention deficit disorder (ADD). Those affected by ADD have great difficulty focusing on a task at hand. I know I must have had this as a child, but I'm glad they didn't know how to treat it back then. I wanted always to stay in high gear!

I am convinced that many Christians have what I call SADD—spiritual attention deficit disorder. They can't seem to concentrate on prayer or Bible study. They find it difficult to serve others. Beyond the spiritual disciplines, they can't maintain a focus on thinking, speaking, and acting honestly with pure motives. In other words, it's a huge challenge for them to maintain a focus on God's goodness in their lives.

Goodness grows out of righteous integrity. The person who manifests God's goodness thinks good thoughts, speaks good words, and performs good deeds. What the person thinks lines up with what he speaks, and what he speaks lines up with what he does. He is consistent in the integrity of his life.

Those who suffer from SADD, however, are hit-and-miss in the goodness they manifest. The Enemy of all that is godly and genuinely good, Satan, has directed Christians away from the path of goodness through his lies and deception.

THE FOES OF GOODNESS

We no longer live in a straightforward world. Instead, our society swirls with lies and deception. Rarely do we call a lie a lie, of course. We use fancy words such as *double-talk* or *spin mastering*. We are adding another layer of deception to what is already rank deception!

Rarely, too, do we directly name the work and influence of Satan as evil. We try to put a good face on evil so as not to hurt anyone's feelings. But in the pure light of God's goodness, a lie is a lie and deception is deception. Lying and deception in all their forms bring us to the root of evil.

Jesus called the devil "a liar and the father of lies" (John 8:44). The devil's nature is absolute evil, but he is smart enough to cloak his identity through deception. The Scripture tells us that the Evil One masquerades as an angel of light in order to deceive as many as possible (see 2 Corinthians 11:14). He puts on a cloak of goodness in an attempt to mask his real nature.

Just as the devil does not want to *appear* to be evil, neither do those who commit evil deeds in our world. Evildoers tend to operate under the cloak of darkness or in a disguise. Evil presents one appearance on the surface but has a different character underneath.

Self-justification and excuse making are employed to hide evil. A woman walks out on her family, and to put a good face on her behavior, she rationalizes her sin. "I owe it to myself to be happy, and since I'm not happy in this marriage, my decision to leave is the right one." A person may drink to excess and try to put a good face on his behavior. "I have so many problems, I need to forget my troubles," he tells others. "Alcohol helps ease the pain and sorrow."

A person may be very blessed of God but then fail to give back to God's work out of the riches she receives from the Lord. To put a good face on her lack of generosity, she may say, "I'm going to keep on investing my money so I can make even more. Then I'll be able to give more money to the Lord's work."

These are nothing more than excuses, self-deception, and lies. The person who abandons his family does not become happier; he nearly always lives to deeply regret that day. Alcohol never *really* eases a person's pain or sorrow, and the person who fails to give to the Lord nearly always loses not only what she should have given away, but even more. The fruit of unrighteous behavior is always evil—the person who engages in such behaviors ends up diminished, diseased, and destroyed. And he nearly always takes someone else with him into sorrow and destruction.

THE LIE OF THE FLESH

Paul not only described the fruit of the Holy Spirit, he also described the "works of the flesh" (Galatians 5:19, KJV), called in the *New International Version* "the acts of the sinful nature." Among these acts he cited "sexual immorality, impurity and debauchery; idolatry and witchcraft; hatred, discord, jealousy, fits of rage, selfish ambition, dissensions, factions and envy; drunkenness, orgies, and the like" (Galatians 5:19-21). Paul said very plainly, "I warn you, as I did before, that those who live like this will not inherit the kingdom of God" (Galatians 5:21).

As we have seen with the work of Satan, at the root of *all* works of the flesh are a series of lies. Here are a few of them:

- *Pursue the habit of sexual immorality, and you will find love while enjoying an exciting time.* Evil hides the truth that you will likely have your heart broken and will have a very good chance of contracting a devastating disease.

- *Engage in a life of drinking and partying to the point of drunkenness, and you will experience excitement and an end to your dull existence.* I don't have to tell you about the lives and families that are devastated by drunken drivers and by having someone they love destroy his or her life with alcohol.

- *Engage in acts of discord, jealousy, or anger, and others will realize they must respect you and yield to you. You will have things done your way.* Again, all lies. No one truly respects a bully or a gossip.

As Satan promotes the works of the flesh, he tells you a half-truth. Yes, a life of drinking and partying might initially bring you fun and a degree of excitement. But Satan carefully avoids adding the full truth of "but not for long." His deception succeeds in pointing out the temporary thrill of the moment, the immediate gratification of one's impulses, but the Father of Lies never tells the truth about the eventual destruction that you will suffer due to the works of the flesh.

THE DEVASTATING WORK OF SATAN'S LIES

Lies and deception fragment our lives. We are torn between what we do and what we should do. It is always Satan's purpose to separate us from God and to divide us from one another. It is his purpose to create disharmony in our emotions, thoughts, and motives. The works of the flesh create confusion over what is right and wrong. The works of the flesh cause a division in our relationships, bringing about distrust and alienation.

This division between people begins on a personal level but quickly grows to consume an entire society. The works of the flesh create a deep gap between those who desire the righteousness of God and those who seek to live according to their own definitions of good and evil. Among those who routinely engage in the works of the flesh, there are no unifying principles, and there is no unifying character of high moral and ethical standards. Those who promote the works of evil are divided both internally and among themselves.

In sharp contrast, the fruit of the Holy Spirit is a united and interrelated cluster of character traits, like seeds of a pomegranate encased in the skin of the fruit. Those who practice true spirituality enjoy an integrated, harmonious life. Those who are Spirit-sealed, Spirit-filled, and Spirit-led do not have scattered emotions or divided loyalties. They are whole men and women, simply because they have discovered the true spirituality that heals.

DIVISION LEADS TO DESTRUCTION

Military strategists know that the surest way to subdue an opponent is not to rely on a frontal attack. Instead, you undermine an enemy by creating internal division. If you want to destroy an army, attack the unity of its soldiers. Not only do you seek to divide the troops physically on the battlefield, but you cut off their supply line. You do all you can to separate troops from their leaders, and you employ tactics to undercut morale. If you can create enough dissension, you have a good chance of winning the battle.

Satan uses this tactic against families, churches, and communities. He lures us with activities and behaviors that separate family members from one another. He destroys churches by introducing rumors, jealousy, and disputes over doctrine, worship, or ministry focus.

Jesus identified this process when He described Satan's nature. He said, "The thief comes only to steal and kill and destroy" (John 10:10). These three actions give a fairly comprehensive definition of the face of evil. None of us would call stealing, killing, and destruction "good." Evil must be labeled for what it is: *evil.* It is in the opposite of these acts of Satan that we find goodness.

THE NATURE OF GOODNESS

The Greek word for *pure* and *sincere* is *agathos.* This is goodness that springs forth in Christlike actions toward others. *Agathos* is characterized by honesty, truthfulness, and blazing integrity. *Agathos* is "a desire to help and comfort, to encourage and motivate." The goodness of God builds up a person or an organization and promotes wholeness in a person or community. Unlike evil, which is fragmented and can work at odds with itself, God's goodness is always unified, never competing against itself. God's goodness is pervasive, impacting every area of our life.

Our Thoughts

Goodness causes us to focus on what is good in another person's life. The apostle Paul wrote about this to the Philippians: "Whatever is true, whatever is noble, whatever is right, whatever is pure, whatever is lovely, whatever is admirable—if anything is excellent or praiseworthy—think about such things" (Philippians 4:8). We are to capture our thoughts, turning them toward the goodness of God.

But, you may be thinking, *everywhere we turn, the news is filled with appalling crimes, horrible disasters, and devastating disease. To think about only those things that are noble, right, pure, lovely, and admirable is to live in a fantasy land.*

Not at all! To choose to think about the things that are excellent and praiseworthy is to fix our thoughts on God, who controls this world and who is the Victor over evil. We can choose to focus on the bad we see all around us, or we can choose to focus on the good we see in God and in His people.

When we focus on evil, we can easily become consumed with dread and cynicism. We close ourselves off from other people. Those who hold these feelings inside and who isolate themselves become discouraged and depressed. This is never an outcome that brings healing.

On the other hand, when we focus on the goodness of God, we find hope and encouragement. Faith rises up in us. When we choose to see the best in others, we are more open to them. We are willing to work together to achieve goals. And if we remain focused on the goodness of the work that God has called us to do, we find a deep sense of fulfillment, purpose, and satisfaction. This is tangible evidence of God's healing spirituality at work.

Choosing to think good thoughts is the frame of mind that God's Spirit manifests in us. God wants us to fall asleep in peace at night. He wants us to be positive about what He is doing and eagerly expectant about what He has planned for us today, tomorrow, and in eternity. This goodness is the very nature of God! He is not discouraged or despondent about evil. He is saddened by it, but He is not the least bit thwarted in His work. He takes delight in His people. He experiences the joy of His creation. He knows the pleasure of communicating with His children and of planning blessings for His people. God is good, and what He thinks is good.

Too many of us see God as serious and stern in judgment. Our God is a joyful God, a God of gladness. The Bible says He rejoices over His children (see Isaiah 62:5; Matthew 18:13-14). God is the Author of all things noble, right, pure, lovely, praiseworthy. He delights in all that operates according to the way He created it. When we focus on God's goodness, we will find that our own thoughts will become good.

Our Speech

Goodness changes the way we speak. This does not mean we simply give up cursing and other improper language. It isn't limited to a commitment to stop telling off-color or bigoted jokes. It doesn't mean that we promise to end all gossip. Certainly, the person who is manifesting the goodness of God's Spirit will not engage in such speech. Good speech, however, goes far beyond the elimination of certain words.

Most of us had mothers who taught us: "If you can't say something good, don't say anything at all." That was good advice! The Bible calls us to speak good to and about other people. Jesus even said we are to speak well of our enemies (see Luke 6:27-28). That's the last thing most of us want to do! When people spread lies about us, our first impulse is to speak ill of them or defend ourselves while declaring them to be liars.

That is the impulse of our fleshly nature. The Bible calls us, instead, to use our speech to bless others. This means to put them in "proper position" before God—with God as sovereign and the person as subject to God. It means to say something that will put them in the position of receiving good from God.

Think for a moment of what it is that you truly want God to pour out on another person. What does the other person need most? The person who spews hatred doesn't need more hatred spewed back at him. He needs a serious dose of God's love poured out on his life so that he knows without a doubt that God cares for him and seeks to establish a relationship with him. The person who erupts in anger doesn't need an angry response—that only creates more anger in her soul. She needs a serious dose of assurance that God is at work on her behalf. She needs encouragement to trust God and to believe that God can be relied upon to bring about justice and restoration. Our speech becomes good when we truly want the goodness of God to be manifested toward another person.

Our Emotional Responses

Goodness impacts our behavior toward others, including our emotional response. When we respond in hatred, anger, or bitterness—or when we set out to undercut or defame others—we want to keep them at a distance. We want them out of our lives.

I have met people who lived in dread of seeing another person to the point where they stopped coming to church, just in case that person might show up. They were constantly looking over their shoulder to see if the other person had walked into the store in which they were shopping. What a terrible way to live!

Jesus said to His disciples:

> Love your enemies, do good to those who hate you…pray
> for those who mistreat you. If someone strikes you on one
> cheek, turn to him the other also. If someone takes your
> cloak, do not stop him from taking your tunic. Give to
> everyone who asks you, and if anyone takes what belongs

to you, do not demand it back. Do to others as you would
have them do to you. (Luke 6:27-31)

What a high standard Jesus set! High, but entirely doable in the power
of the Holy Spirit.

THE WORK OF THE SPIRIT

How is it that we can love our enemies, pray for those who mistreat us,
and respond with goodness to those who make unreasonable demands?
We can't take the path of goodness unless the Spirit of God constantly fills
us with true spirituality. Here is how the Spirit works in us to accomplish
His goodness.

Seeing the Root of Evil

The Holy Spirit challenges us to see another person's actions in a new
light. The harm that another person commits is not only against us, it is
against God as well. Deep inside, what the hurtful person is reacting
against is very likely the reflection of God at work in our lives. They resent
our relationships, our blessings, our stature in character. They hate the fact
that we may have influenced people around them or stood up for what
they intuitively know to be the truth they have rejected. So they lash out.
We must see their behavior as an attempt to lash out at God, not at us.

Emulating Jesus

The Holy Spirit leads us to ask: "How would God respond? If this person
had treated Jesus as he treated me or spoken to Jesus the way he spoke to
me, how would Jesus have responded?" We know that Jesus would have

spoken loving words. He would have turned the other cheek. As we seek to do what Jesus would have done, the Holy Spirit empowers us to do good to a person who has hurt us.

That does not mean, of course, that we are to avoid rebuking someone if such a need arises. Sometimes confronting a lie or wrong behavior is the most loving thing we can do. Jesus admonished the hypocritical Pharisees, but not because He hated them. He hated what they were doing and saying. He loved them—and those who were following their teachings—enough to challenge their errors. Giving to a person can mean giving a word of truth to counteract a lie.

Doing Good to Our Persecutors

When we do good to those who hate and misuse us, two amazing things happen. First, the other person's hatred is defused. The Bible tells us:

> Do not repay anyone evil for evil. Be careful to do what is right in the eyes of everybody. If it is possible, as far as it depends on you, live at peace with everyone. Do not take revenge, my friends, but leave room for God's wrath, for it is written: "It is mine to avenge; I will repay," says the Lord. On the contrary:
>
> If your enemy is hungry, feed him;
>   if he is thirsty, give him something to drink.
> In doing this, you will heap burning coals on his head.
>
> Do not be overcome by evil, but overcome evil with good.
> (Romans 12:17-21)

Good overcomes evil every time—perhaps not immediately, but eventually in God's ultimate working of good. It is perhaps not in a way we can experience, but in God's working things for *our* good on the basis of the way we treated the other person. Good wins out!

Our manifesting goodness to a person who has hurt us puts the burden of response on the other person. Most people who have willfully caused pain find a response of goodness to be very unsettling. They are befuddled when a Christian responds with good rather than by fighting back.

The Spirit-led response of showing goodness rather than spite also touches those who surround the wrongdoer. The actions of goodness lead others to question: "Why are you picking on that person? What purpose is there in pursuing hatred?" The cohorts of the person who has done evil tend to wander away, leaving the wrongdoer isolated.

In many cases, the evildoer will find that he cannot resist an act of kindness. He often finds himself under conviction and is forced to confront his own evil. He will seek to reconcile or make amends with the person he has hurt. Our goodness provides an opportunity for the Spirit of God to work in another person's life as well as in our own. Thus, the spiritual fruit of goodness brings healing to two people.

A Change in Our Heart

When we respond to a wrongdoer with goodness, God has an opportunity to move in our lives to heal us emotionally from the wounds that have been inflicted. He rewards our reflection of His own character with strength, compassion, and genuine feelings of love for the evildoer. These are signs of His fruit being borne out in our lives.

And in the end, our manifestation of goodness toward an evildoer creates a greater awareness in us of God's goodness. We see more that is right about God's ways. We see more that is worthy of praise. We see more ways of bringing honor to His name. We see more ways to reach out to others with the tremendous news, "God is good—all the time, in all situations. God desires good for you, and He is working for your good even now."

THE HUMAN SPIRIT

The Source of all power both to resist evil and to keep God's commandments is the Holy Spirit. He empowers us to recognize Satan's lies, to stand against Satan's deceit, and to resist Satan's temptations. As the Spirit of Truth, He leads us into all truth.

You may be asking, "Michael, are you saying that I have no will, no power, no ability? Is my human spirit of no value?"

Not at all. The spirit within us is capable of making choices, establishing plans, and feeling emotions. The human spirit is integrally linked to our ability to learn, change, and motivate ourselves to act. Our human spirit is the seat of the human will.

The prevailing opinion of shadow spirituality seems to be this: A person can do all sorts of evil but still be a "good person in his heart of hearts." A mother can kill her children but be a "good person" who is just mentally ill. A father can abandon his family and fail to support them but be a "good person" who is just stressed out. A teenager can steal but still be labeled a "good kid" who just had some bad breaks.

Evil deeds flow from an evil heart. Jesus said, "By their fruit you will recognize them" (Matthew 7:20). What willfully *chooses* evil *is* evil. Mental and emotional illness may contribute to the evil behavior. An inability to handle life's stress may contribute. But at some point, a person *decides* to embark on a path that results in evil deeds. Those who continue to engage in sinful activities cannot display a godly character. It is not possible for a Spirit-led, Spirit-filled, Spirit-sealed person to choose to engage routinely in the behaviors associated with a sinful nature and *be* loving, peaceful, joyful, patient, kind, good, faithful, gentle, and self-controlled. The behaviors born of a sinful nature and the character qualities of the Holy Spirit are completely incompatible. God has given us the ability to make our own choices, and with God's help we can make the choice for good.

The foremost act we can carry out with our human will is to fall on our faces before God and say with great humility, "I have made a bad choice. Forgive me. Cleanse me. Restore me. Help me." We must never say, "I can do this by myself." We must never assume, "I don't need to consult God on this." We are capable of manifesting goodness only because He imparts His goodness to us.

The story is told of a beggar who stopped a businessman on a downtown street and asked him for a quarter. The businessman took a careful look at the beggar's unshaven face and asked, "Don't I know you from somewhere?"

The beggar replied, "Yes. I am your former classmate. We studied together in college."

The businessman responded, "Why, Sam, of course I know you!" And without another word, he pulled out his checkbook and wrote a check for one hundred dollars. "Take this and make a new start with your life," the businessman told the beggar. "I don't care what has happened in your past. It is your future that counts."

Tears welled up in the beggar's eyes as he walked toward a nearby bank. He looked through the door and saw the spotless interior and the well-dressed tellers. He saw his own filthy rags and thought, *They'll swear that I forged this check. They won't hand over that much money.* He turned and walked away.

The next day, the beggar and the businessman ran into each other again. The businessman asked, "Sam, what did you do with my check?" He secretly feared that the man had used it for alcohol or had gambled it away.

The beggar pulled the check from his dirty shirt pocket and admitted that he hadn't gone into the bank. The businessman looked him in the eye and said, "Listen, my friend, what makes that check good is not your clothes or your appearance. It's my signature that makes that check good. Go immediately and cash it."

Many of us, like that beggar, have given up hope. We are likely to look at the spiritual fruit of goodness and assume that we will never attain it. And in our own power, we never will. It is only when we look to God and say, "Fill me today and help me express Your goodness" that we are able to confront evil and overcome it. It is only because of His signature on our lives—a signature written on our hearts with the blood of Jesus—that we are able to keep His commandments, take every thought captive, and speak as the Holy Spirit gives us the words.

True spirituality heals our weakness and empowers us to manifest the very goodness of God.

Eleven

THE HEALING POWER
OF GOD'S FAITHFULNESS

Trust Grows As Promises Are Kept

George MacDonald, a famous British author of the nineteenth century, once said, "To be trusted is a greater compliment than to be loved."[1] When I first saw this quotation, I objected to it. But the more I pondered it, the more I found myself in total agreement. Love is subject to so many emotional interpretations, so many highs and lows. Trust is steady and constant. It is a positioning of the will and affection that endures.

Alas, trustworthiness is no longer a trait that is universally held in high esteem. Gone are the days when a promise was a promise, when a person's word was his bond.

Likewise, *faithfulness* is considered to be so old-fashioned that it has all but been taken out of circulation. "Faithful" is far more likely to be ascribed to a favorite pet than to a spouse, far more likely to be linked to a geyser than a political leader, and on those rare occasions when it is associated with a person, we are quicker to refer to a faithful friend than a faithful God.

Faithfulness is rooted in commitment, and therein lies a big part of the problem with our culture's general loss of this virtue. Shadow spirituality is committed to political expediency, private gain, enhancing one's personal glory, and seeking self-gratification.

But in God's kingdom, faithfulness stands at the heart of who God is and what He wants to do in and through us. As an aspect of true spirituality, it is the lifeblood of all lasting relationships. A lack of faithfulness leads quickly to disintegration, disharmony, and eventually to the demise of a relationship.

TRUST GROWS FROM KEEPING PROMISES

Faithfulness is rooted in trust. Trust is produced when we make a promise and then keep it, when we make a commitment and then honor it, when we say something and mean it.

What would it be like if you sent your children to school tomorrow morning and none of the teachers showed up because they didn't feel like going to work? What would it be like if you went to church this Sunday and found that the pastoral staff had gone fishing because they wanted a break? What would it be like if you went to your bank on a Tuesday morning and discovered that the doors were closed because the workers had taken a day off to run personal errands? To a great extent our society runs on the concept of faithfulness even while losing a personal adherence to this trait. Consistency, reliability, and proven track records are all aspects of faithfulness.

Evidence of God's faithfulness is all around us. God always shows up. He always loves. He always forgives repentant sinners. He always accomplishes His plans and fulfills His purposes.

Jesus' disciples could count on Him to be faithful. Every time they were in dire danger or desperate need, Jesus was there for them. He was true to His Word; He kept His promises. Jesus came to His disciples with words of comfort and assurance, even if it meant walking on water or appearing in a room that was sealed with locked doors and barred windows. Even when it meant walking out of a rock-sealed and heavily guarded tomb.

Just as Jesus can be counted on to keep His word, the Holy Spirit is faithful to us. Jesus said of the Holy Spirit, "He lives with you and will be in you. I will not leave you as orphans; I will come to you" (John 14:17-18). The Holy Spirit *never* leaves or forsakes those who have accepted Jesus as their Savior. He is present with us always.

Of course there are times when we do not feel the presence of God. We may not feel close to God or sense that He is at work. Regardless of our feelings, though, God is with us. Most of the time when we do not have an awareness of God's presence, we are the ones who have moved away.

It's a little like the man who courted a woman, and whenever they rode in his car, the woman sat so close to her boyfriend that it was difficult to tell if the car carried one person or two.

After the couple had been married awhile, the two were out driving. The wife was sitting on her side of the car, the husband was behind the wheel, and the wife said, "Honey, it doesn't seem as if we are as close as we once were." The husband looked over at his wife and said, "I haven't moved."

So, too, with God. We often don't feel His presence with us because we are the ones who have moved away from Him in our neglect, indifference, undisciplined behavior, and even sin.

Apart from our behavior, however, our feelings are often fickle. Emotions rise and fall. They are never a good gauge for determining God's presence. God is with us because He said He would be with us, not because we feel his nearness. One of the last things Jesus said to His disciples was, "Surely I am with you always, to the very end of the age" (Matthew 28:20).

FAITHFULNESS MEANS GIVING YOUR BEST

Faithfulness means far more than just showing up, of course. It means giving your best to any effort that you undertake. Contrast that with the attitude of a hitchhiker. As he stands at the side of the road, extending his arm with an upturned thumb, he is saying to the passing motorists: "You furnish the gas and a safe, dependable car, take care of the insurance and maintenance, and I'll just ride for free." The hitchhiker is a rider, not a provider. He is not giving his best to the situation; he is simply benefiting from the efforts of another.

The faithful person is not a rider but a provider—a person who helps make things happen. Our churches have too many hitchhikers. They attend a Sunday-morning service, but they say in essence: "The rest of you can serve in the various ministries, give generously to fund the operating budget, teach the Sunday-school classes, and participate in evangelistic outreaches." They just go along for the ride, but because they attend Sunday services, they believe they are being faithful to the Lord.

Hardly.

To be faithful means to cling as closely as you can to the things you know to be right to do. The person who walks as close to the edge of the cliff as possible but still claims to be on solid ground is not a provider. He is flirting with sin while claiming to be righteous. He may be a child of God, but he is not *filled* with the Holy Spirit, because if he were he would be faithful in every way he knows to be faithful.

VITAL ASPECTS OF FAITHFULNESS

When we think about faithfulness, it's easy to overlook two vital factors. First, we must be faithful in all areas of life—things little and big, seemingly unimportant and important. Second, we must be faithful even when we do not receive an immediate reward.

Faithful in the Little Things

Being faithful in the little things means we keep appointments, follow through on projects, and keep our promises—the small ones as well as large ones.

Faithfulness in the small things extends to marriage. Most people define faithfulness in marriage in terms of sexual fidelity, but faithfulness means far more. It means that you build up and encourage your spouse; you appreciate and applaud your spouse. It means that you make decisions with your spouse's highest good in mind, not your own selfish desire.

Faithfulness in marriage means that you don't spend money on things you have agreed not to spend money on and that you "love, honor, and cherish" your spouse in the way you speak to her. It means you treat your spouse at home the same way you treat your spouse in public.

Faithfulness on the job means doing your best work even when no one is watching. It means showing up on time, putting in a full day's work, and giving your best ideas and creativity and energy to every task. Faithfulness means using company resources wisely. Faithfulness means giving your best effort even if you are not rewarded or even acknowledged. Remember the words of Jesus: "Whoever can be trusted with very little can also be trusted with much, and whoever is dishonest with very little will also be dishonest with much" (Luke 16:10).

Faithful Without Promise of Reward

When we work hard and succeed or sacrificially put others ahead of ourselves, we often feel that we deserve reward and recognition. But we should never allow a lack of reward to keep us from remaining faithful.

In the 1990s many people became accustomed to high returns on their stock investments, with some companies seeing their value double overnight as they went public. We became a nation that expected high reward, often for very little investment of effort. But that period of high growth was temporary. The truth about life on earth is that most people receive very few, if any, great rewards. Most of the good things we do go unheralded. It is easy to conclude that our work is *under*valued and *under*compensated. When we become discouraged over a lack of recognition, we are failing to see that God is a God of both earthly blessings and *eternal* rewards. Nothing we do for His name's sake goes unrewarded in the scope of eternity. The Lord asks us to be patient, to endure, to be faithful in our responsibilities and the humdrum details that hardly seem worth our attention.

Steve Farrar has a wonderful illustration in his book *Finishing Strong*. He asks his readers to imagine a hypothetical scene in first-century Jerusalem, just a decade or two after Jesus was crucified. Suppose people of that time were asked at random, "Who of your generation will people likely remember two thousand years from now?" Most of those surveyed likely would have said Caesar. A few might have named Herod. A few might even have named the high priest of the day.[2]

If you asked a follow-up question, "What about these people known as Christians? Do you think anybody will remember them or their leaders?" the answer would likely have been a cynical smile. "You've got to be kidding? They're a bunch of nobodies. Their leaders keep ending up in jail. People won't remember them next year, much less two thousand years from now."

The world *cannot* value the work that we do to extend God's kingdom. The world simply cannot see the big picture of eternity or the long view of what God is accomplishing on this earth. If you expect praise from the world you'll be disappointed. For that matter, don't expect rewards from other believers. Very few people can even begin to see others as God sees them.

THE FOES OF FAITHFULNESS

Faithfulness runs so counter to the way of the world that we each must guard it closely and uphold it constantly. Three things can diminish our faithfulness very quickly. We must be diligent in guarding against the foes of faithfulness: marginalization of relationship, compromise of truth, and indifference to God's Word.

Marginalizing Our Relationship with God

When we marginalize something, we put it on the fringe of our life. We consider it, at times, to be the icing on the cake, not the cake itself.

Millions of people around the world, including Christians, marginalize God, His work, and their relationship with Him. They think of God only when they have a problem or a pressing need. They attend church only when they feel the need to do something good to win God's approval. They support God's work only when they have a little extra cash or a little extra time. They do not see their relationship with Jesus Christ as involving the whole of life or as the most important relationship in life. The concept of a deep, ongoing relationship with God doesn't even create a blip on their life's radar screen!

God's faithfulness is not a fringe issue. It is not peripheral to our lives. God's faithfulness is abiding, not merely exercised when it is convenient for God. And His faithfulness is not dependent on our faithfulness—His faithfulness is part of His very being. It is a combination of His power and love that cannot be hindered or stopped, contradicted or reversed.

This is a high standard indeed. And consider that God calls us to be faithful to Him just as He is faithful to us. He wants to be the Lord of our lives, not just an occasional acquaintance. He desires to have an intimate, enduring, constant, all-encompassing relationship with us.

How can we be faithful to God and to others just as He is to us? We begin by never marginalizing our relationship with God. When we try to push Him to the fringes, we are rejecting and ignoring God. The result is a drastic diminishing of our faithfulness.

Do you truly want the fruit of the Spirit? Then get to know the character of God by talking to Him and listening to Him on a daily basis. Martin Luther said, "Whoever knows that God is gracious to him walks through life along the path of roses, even in tribulation, and for him the land flows with milk and honey."

Compromising God's Truth

A second thing that diminishes our faithfulness is when we compromise God's truth. Anytime we read a command or requirement in Scripture and conclude, "Well, I can see what it says, but I don't think that's what God really meant," or "That may be what God said to the people of that society, but those aren't God's words for me today," we are compromising

God's truth. We are saying that God wavers. If the definitions and meanings of God's Word are forever shifting, how can a person ever know *which* aspects of God's Word are eternally true and can be trusted?

Anytime we alter, adjust, or edit aspects of God's Word to suit our own purposes or understanding, we err greatly. And not only that, we diminish our ability to rely upon the faithfulness of God.

Those who compromise the truth of God's Word, of course, also diminish their own motivation to be faithful and their own ability to be faithful. No thoughtful person desires to follow or work alongside someone who cannot be trusted. Instead, we are drawn to friends, coworkers, and others we can count on. We want to associate with people who will be steadfast in their love and who will keep their commitments. If we see God as someone who changes His mind or who is capricious in His judgments, we will have little desire to follow Him.

If you do not understand what God's Word means, ask the Lord. If you have questions, seek answers. Jesus said, "Everyone who asks receives; he who seeks finds; and to him who knocks, the door will be opened" (Matthew 7:8). One of the great miracles of being filled with God's Spirit is that we gain a growing understanding of God's Word.

The British parliamentarian William Wilberforce, who single-handedly pushed through England's antislavery bill, was a close friend of William Pitt, one of the great prime ministers of England. Being a godly man, Wilberforce prayed for his friend's salvation and faithfully tried to witness to his friend of Christ's love and free offer of salvation—all to no avail. Wilberforce believed that if he could just get Pitt to a service where he might hear a preacher named Richard Cecil, he would be converted. After months of invitations, Pitt finally agreed to hear Cecil preach.

Richard Cecil preached the gospel clearly and reverently. Wilberforce was ecstatic, sure that Pitt, a brilliant man, would fully grasp the central message of the gospel as Cecil had preached it.

No sooner had the two friends walked outside the church than Pitt said to Wilberforce, "I did not understand a word of what this man was talking about."[3] No less an intellect than Prime Minister William Pitt failed to grasp the simple message of the gospel because he did not have the Holy Spirit opening his eyes to the truth. Having not surrendered his life to Christ, Pitt had no spiritual understanding. It is the Holy Spirit who quickens our minds to understand the Word of God.

Indifference to God's Word

The prophet Amos cried out:

> "The days are coming," declares the Sovereign LORD,
>   "when I will send a famine through the land—
> not a famine of food or a thirst for water,
>   but a famine of hearing the words of the LORD.
> Men will stagger from sea to sea,
>   and wander from north to east,
> searching for the word of the LORD,
>   but they will not find it." (Amos 8:11-12)

I have no doubt that we are living in the day Amos described hundreds of years ago. There are some Christians who have a burning, ever-searching hunger for God's Word, but that is not the norm across the churches of our nation.

In many ways, we have replaced the mourner's bench and the black leather Bible with a psychiatrist's couch. We have exalted preachers whose words make people *feel* good instead of helping us *be* good. We have rated our churches according to their size rather than their holy fervor for God's truth.

Visit the huge cathedrals of England and Scotland, and you are likely to see fewer than twenty people gathered on Sunday morning. Go to Germany or Holland—nations that were so prominent in the Reformation—and see how few worshipers populate the huge cathedrals.

When we become indifferent to God's Word, including God's command through Jesus that we take the gospel to all people in all nations, we diminish our capacity to be faithful. We lose our zeal, our ardor, our "first love," our deep desire to stand up for the truth and witness to the lost.

Those who are authentically filled with God's Spirit are excited about the things of God. They rejoice at the salvation of lost souls. They delight in seeing God at work. They are enthusiastically eager to worship God and serve Him.

Those who are genuinely faithful are those who:

- *Pursue their personal relationship with the Lord.* They spend time with Him, praising and thanking Him, voicing their concerns to Him, confessing their sins to Him, and listening to what He speaks to them from His Word. God's Word says, "Let us draw near to God with a sincere heart in full assurance of faith" (Hebrews 10:22).

- *Desire to know God's truth.* They seek to grow in their understanding of God's principles, purposes, and promises. They desire to keep the commandments of God, so they read and study God's Word in order to know the commandments. They draw upon God's Word for hope and motivation. God's Word says, "Let us hold unswerving to the hope we profess" (Hebrews 10:23).

- *Continue in fellowship with other believers.* Those who are faithful keep going to church even when they don't feel like it or are criticized by others for attending regularly. They choose to be in relationship with other believers, drawing strength from them and giving to them. God's Word says, "Let us consider how we may spur one another on toward love and good deeds. Let us not give up meeting together...but let us encourage one another" (Hebrews 10:24-25).

FAITHFULNESS BRINGS US TO WHOLENESS

Healing is a process—none of us are made truly whole in a day. God works in our lives, molding us bit by bit into the character-likeness of Christ Jesus. The Holy Spirit heals our memories one relationship or one experience at a time. He confronts and deals with us regarding our sins, one at a time. He addresses our bad habits, our lack of knowledge or understanding, and He does it one issue at a time.

For our healing to continue moving forward, certain things need to be done with consistency.

We all know this in our physical lives. One full day of exercise is not the same as thirty minutes of exercise a few times a week. One day of dieting does not make us thin. One day of eating properly coupled with one good night of sleep does not restore our health. It is not what we do *some* of the time that causes ill health or creates good health—it's what we do most of the time.

The same is true for our emotional and relational life. It's not the way we love a parent, spouse, or child on one occasion that counts. The one time we showed up for a child's performance quickly fades in memory. It's what we do day in and day out that counts.

The same is true for our spiritual life. Reading the Bible for an hour once a month isn't nearly as beneficial as reading the Bible ten minutes a day for a month. Praying only when we have a pressing need isn't as spiritually beneficial as setting aside time every day to praise, thank, petition, and worship God. Being involved in a ministry once a year doesn't have the same impact on us as being involved in that ministry on a weekly basis. In all areas of our lives, it's what we do consistently, faithfully, and diligently that reaps benefits and produces wholeness in us.

God is faithful *always*. He does not change (see Hebrews 13:8). Because He is faithful, we can have the assurance of salvation. We can *know* that we have the gift of eternal life. We can *know* the Holy Spirit is in us and with us always. We can *know* that God hears and answers prayer. We can *know* that God rewards those who earnestly seek Him (see Hebrews 11:6). The person who lives with that kind of assurance is a person who feels secure and purposeful and hopeful. He has a deep and abiding confidence that cannot be shaken.

Recently, a friend of mine shared an encounter she had with a friend from high school. They had once been active in the same church youth group. She saw this friend again after years at a high-school reunion party and was shocked at his appearance. She discovered that he had turned his back on God and now considered himself to be an atheist. Not only that, but he had been HIV positive for more than a decade. He proudly informed her that the doctors were amazed he was still alive, and then he laughed, "I'm amazed as well."

This woman felt a strong conviction that she needed to talk further with him, and the man agreed to have lunch with her. When they got together, she learned that he was taking more than a dozen prescriptions for various health problems, was in counseling twice a week, and that he had very few friends. He did not, however, want to talk about God.

Finally, the woman said to him, "Tom, look at the evidence all around you. If I am wrong in believing what I believe—if all that I hold to be true about Jesus isn't true, and if there is no heaven or hell at the end of this life—let me share that I am glad I believe what I believe. I sleep peacefully at night, with great assurance that if I die before I awaken, I will be with Jesus. I have purpose, joy, and a sense of fulfillment. I have wonderful friends who also have a spiritual life rooted in Christ Jesus as their Savior. I have a fabulous feeling inside that I have been cleansed of my sin; I don't live in guilt or shame or regret. My life is marked by health, and I know that God is making me more whole every day. I have evidence every day that God is faithful to me and present in my life. "

"Well," Tom responded, "I have clear evidence that God is *not* faithful to me."

"No," the woman boldly countered. "It seems to me that God has been *very* faithful in keeping you alive against all the odds for the last fifteen years. You are the one who has not been faithful to Him."

Faithfulness produces a deep assurance that we are connected to God with a bond that cannot be broken and that extends into eternity. Faithfulness produces in us a deep knowing that what we say and do under the guidance of the Holy Spirit will yield a harvest in God's kingdom. Faithfulness produces a deep security that manifests itself in courage, confidence, strength of character, and wholeness. God's faithfulness to us leads to our faithfulness to Him and to others. And ultimately, His faithfulness heals us.

Twelve

THE HEALING POWER
OF GOD'S GENTLENESS

The Lord's Meekness Is a Far Cry from Weakness

One of the most difficult tasks we face is the challenge of correcting a wrong perception. Most of us operate from the position, "I've made up my mind; don't confuse me with the facts." In other words, perception is reality.

One perception that many Christians hold in error, however, is their perception of what it means to be meek. In the description of the fruit of the Spirit in Galatians 5:22-23, some Bible versions translate the spiritual fruit of gentleness as *meekness*. This is actually an enlightening translation of the word if you understand the true meaning of meekness. But both outside the church and within the church, people think of meekness as weakness or timidity. Those who are meek are thought of as wimps or cowards.

Nothing could be further from the truth. The Greek word for meekness, *praotes*, is synonymous with courage, confidence, security, and strength under control. The Greek philosopher Aristotle had a theory that virtue was held in the balance between two vices. *Praotes*, or meekness, was the virtue that was held in balance between the vice of rage at one extreme, and the vice of indifference at the other extreme.

We have a phrase, "gentle giant," that is similar in meaning to the concept of *praotes*. A gentle giant is big, strong, and easily capable of destruction or rage. However, the gentleness of this person causes him to care for the weak, defend the helpless, and nurture the innocent. A gentle giant is strong in character and resolve, yet tender and humble before God.

Meekness Is Not Weakness

Sadly, our culture confuses weakness and strength. Let me assure you, the man who walks into his house and kicks the cat and reminds everyone that he is the man of the house is the furthest thing from being a man of strength. Likewise, the person who has to remind everyone of her importance is not a strong person. The person who continually seeks honor, brags about his exploits, and protects his own little kingdom is not a strong person.

Moses is described by the Bible as the meekest man on the face of the earth. In some modern translations, the term used is *humble* (see Numbers 12:3). If you have studied the life of Moses, you know already that he was anything but weak or cowardly. Moses was a strong and decisive leader. He was prone to lose his temper, even to the point of killing a person he regarded as committing an injustice, and whacking a rock instead of speaking to it as God commanded. There was nothing milquetoast about Moses!

Moses was a man who was also completely yielded to God. He stood in humble awe before God. He had compassion for the children of Israel, even when they were disobedient and rebellious, and he was on the verge of losing his temper. He interceded on their behalf.

This great leader was meek as he walked in humility. Today, a meek person leads his family with quiet courage and confidence—never having to remind everybody that he's in charge. The meek person wins an award but sees no reason to tell anybody about it. The meek person is like the member of my church who was given an honorary doctorate. I happened to find out about this award given to him, and I congratulated him. He responded, "Because you are my pastor and my friend, I'm glad you know this, but if you ever tell anybody, I'll stop coming to your church."

Booker T. Washington was a man who knew the meekness of true spirituality. Born in 1856, he worked in the coal mines as a child, taking off only three months a year to attend school. He valued education, however, and worked hard, and eventually he graduated from Hampton Institute. Six years later, at the age of twenty-five, he was appointed the first president of Tuskegee Institute, a trade school for African Americans.

Shortly after Washington accepted this post at Tuskegee, he was walking down an Alabama street when a white woman spotted him and summoned him to come and chop some wood for her. Most of us would never have tolerated such indignity! We might have said to her in anger: "Who do you think you are, lady? How arrogant of you to judge me by the color of my skin. Don't you know who I am?"

But Washington knew about meekness. He took off his coat, chopped some wood for the woman, and carried an armload of it into her house. Later, when the woman discovered who he was and the position he held, she went to his office to apologize. He said to her simply, "It's all right. I delight in doing favors for my friends."

That's true strength under control. That's being a godly gentle giant!

That woman not only became a generous supporter of the Tuskegee Institute, but she left her entire estate to the institute. Washington went on to advise Presidents Theodore Roosevelt and William Howard Taft. He wrote a number of books and became one of the best-known heroes of his day.[1]

A weak man? Never. A meek man? Absolutely!

MEEKNESS IS NOT FALSE MODESTY

As much as meekness stands in opposition to bragging and self-seeking aggrandizement, meekness also stands in opposition to false modesty. I believe false modesty is more dangerous to our character than braggadocio because false modesty is much harder to detect. It looks like meekness, making no claim to talent, ability, or special giftedness. In fact, the person who exhibits false modesty says, in words or mannerisms, "I'm not worthy. I'm not anything. God is everything."

The truth is that God has given each person at least one gift or natural talent. He gives each believer at least one spiritual gift to be used for ministry purposes. He gives to each person a measure of intelligence and a measure of faith.

In gifting us, God is saying, "You are important. You have value to Me. You are My beloved and unique creation. I have redeemed you from the clutches of the devil. And I have a plan and purpose for your life."

Far more than expressing genuine modesty, the person who refuses to own up to any talent is acting in pride. He is claiming to know himself better than God knows him. He is claiming to be nothing when God says he is somebody! He is calling greater attention to himself and less attention to God.

Let me give you two examples: A man makes an excellent speech, and a friend applauds him. The speaker says, "Oh, that was nothing." False modesty! A person is dressed well, and someone gives her a compliment. The person replies, "This old outfit?" False modesty!

A colleague of mine, Ron Ervin, is a great encourager. He often says to me after a sermon, "That was a great message!" My response back to Ron is always the same, "Ron…they all are!"

How can I make such a claim without my words being self-exalting? Because Ron knows that I can take no credit for anything that I have. It is all a gift from God. God gave me the amount of intelligence and the skill that I have. God gave me the opportunities and the motivation to develop the intelligence and skill He gave me. God produces the fruit from the words I preach and the books that I write.

If I fail, my failure is my own—it is a product of my own laziness and lack of fervor. But if I succeed, my success is God's. He is the Author and Finisher of all that He has put into me.

The meek person stands in humility before God, knowing that all he has, all he does, and all he is, he owes to God. God gives him every breath, every heartbeat, every good and productive idea, every second of time, every good opportunity. It is God who provides every nudge of wise counsel and who creates divine appointments and encounters, bringing His people together to accomplish His goals. The meek person knows that he is nothing without God.

At the same time, the meek person knows that *because* of God, she has all things, can do all things, and will accomplish all that God commands her to do. The meek person is accurately humble, claiming that all talent, ability, and success come from God. The meek person lays all accolades at the feet of Jesus and says, "You alone are worthy."

THE DEMEANOR OF TRUE SPIRITUALITY

Meekness is reflected in the *way* we express our convictions. Meekness is revealed in the *manner* in which we stand up for the truth and in the *demeanor* we reflect as we answer our critics or antagonists.

A little girl was once given the assignment to write an essay about the Quakers. She wrote: "Quakers are very meek people who never fight and never answer back. My father is a Quaker, but my mother is not."

How did Moses express his convictions? On one occasion both his brother Aaron and sister Miriam became jealous of his success. They were resentful of the way he exercised authority. They began to criticize him and to solicit the support of others in opposing Moses. They were particularly critical that Moses had married a Cushite woman. Some translations refer to her as an Ethiopian woman. She was not an Israelite, and in all likelihood, she was a black woman.

Moses could have reacted in any number of ways. He could have pulled rank, pointing out that God had chosen him to be the leader, and they were in a position to shut up or ship out. He could have called them names indicative of their reproachful behavior. He could have pointed out to them that if it hadn't been for his leadership, they would still be in slavery. Instead, Moses acted in meekness. He said nothing outwardly and acted out of inner security, not revenge. He acted with confidence in God.

Moses refused to respond to the unwarranted criticism. In fact, if God had not acted on Moses' behalf, we probably would never have read about this incident in the Bible. God called Moses, Aaron, and Miriam to the Tent of Meeting, and once they were there, He spoke sternly to Aaron and

Miriam, reviewing Moses' faithfulness and asking the two complainers: "Why then were you not afraid to speak against my servant Moses?" (Numbers 12:8). The anger of the Lord burned against Aaron and Miriam, and when the cloud of the Lord's presence lifted above the tent, Miriam found that she was leprous; her skin was white like snow. God had responded to her complaint about the darkness of her sister-in-law by making her skin very white!

How did Moses respond? Again, with meekness—the strength of a gentle giant. He could have said, "You got what was coming to you, sister. You have your just reward." Instead, he cried out to God, begging Him to heal her.

How We Manifest Meekness

As is true in manifesting any of the character traits of the Holy Spirit, we must first ask the Holy Spirit to fill us with Himself. He is the One who imparts to us the capacity for meekness. How is it that we are enabled to become God's "gentle giants" in our world today?

A Heart of Thanksgiving

We must rely upon the strength of God and not our own strength. We must continually recognize God as the Source of all that we have and are.

We do this through a continual outpouring of thanksgiving. We acknowledge daily that He is our Provider and our Protector. We thank Him daily for our health, strength, mental capacity, talents, spiritual gifts. We thank Him continually for the opportunities He brings our way and the rewards and blessings He bestows on us.

Seeking to Respond to Life As Jesus Did

We must choose to rely upon the Lord to help us respond to life with gentleness, tenderness, and a quiet spirit. We ask daily for His help to respond to others as Jesus responded. We ask Him to help us say what Jesus would say and do what Jesus would do.

The Holy Spirit points continually to Jesus. The Lord said of the Holy Spirit's work in us:

> He will guide you into all truth. He will not speak on his own; he will speak only what he hears, and he will tell you what is yet to come. He will bring glory to me by taking from what is mine and making it known to you. All that belongs to the Father is mine. That is why I said the Spirit will take from what is mine and make it known to you. (John 16:13-15)

How did Jesus reflect meekness? The Bible describes Jesus as being meek, or in some translations, humble (see Matthew 21:5). Jesus described Himself, saying, "I am gentle and humble in heart" (Matthew 11:29).

Jesus made this statement about Himself after saying, "All things have been committed to me by my Father" (Matthew 11:27). Jesus did only what God the Father revealed to Him, commanded Him, authorized for Him. He was 100 percent obedient to the Father. He stood in humility before the Father to the point of saying in the Garden of Gethsemane, "Not as I will, but as you will" (Matthew 26:39).

Jesus continually pointed others to God the Father. He taught His disciples to pray, "Our Father" (see Luke 11:2, NKJV). He said of His relationship to the Father, "I am the true vine, and my Father is the gardener"

(John 15:1). Because He functioned in full obedience to God the Father, Jesus could say to His disciples, "Anyone who has seen me has seen the Father" (John 14:9).

In like manner the Holy Spirit points continually to Jesus. It is the Holy Spirit who reminds us of the words and deeds of Jesus. The Lord said of the Holy Spirit's work in us: "The Spirit will take from what is mine and make it known to you" (John 16:15).

Jesus stood in humility, strength, meekness, and confidence before God the Father, fully absorbing all that the Father was and doing only what the Father commanded. He yielded all honor and glory to the Father.

The Holy Spirit functions in meekness. He fully declares all that Jesus did and all that Jesus is, and He does in our lives only what Jesus has authorized Him to do. He yields all praise and honor and glory to Jesus Christ and to God the Father.

We manifest the Spirit's likeness as we do the same. We fully declare what Jesus did and who Jesus was and is. We do only what Jesus authorizes us to do and what the Holy Sprit compels and enables us to do, and then we yield all honor and glory to Jesus Christ and to God the Father.

We are meek as Jesus was and is meek. We are meek as the Holy Spirit is meek.

Passing On the Compliment

We must choose to point to the Lord anytime we are acknowledged or applauded in any way. "To God be the glory" should be the first words on our lips.

I heard about a young woman who stood before a large congregation in a magnificent cathedral and sang a beautiful song of praise to God. Her performance, which was truly an act of worship, brought the audience to its feet in thunderous applause—a rare phenomenon in this formal, rather austere cathedral. Rather than acknowledging the applause, this young woman turned and reverently bowed with a deep curtsy before the cross that hung above the altar.

Her act of honor and deep respect said: "To God be the glory. All thanks be to God. It's all about Jesus." These are the responses of the meek.

Interceding for Others

We must choose to pray for others, even as Moses prayed for Miriam to be healed. I have no doubt that those who are truly meek make the most powerful prayer intercessors. Indeed, intercession is a hallmark of meekness.

Leonard Ravenhill has aptly pointed out that the church is spiritually anemic and insipid, saying:

> We have many organizers, but few agonizers.
> Many players and payers, but few prayers.
> Many singers, but few clingers.
> Many pastors, but few wrestlers.
> Many fears, but few tears.
> Much fashion, but little passion.
> Many interferers, but few intercessors.
> Failing here, we fail everywhere.[2]

How do I know that intercession is the foremost activity of the meek? Because that is what Jesus is doing for us right now. He is seated at the right hand of the Father, interceding for us, bringing all our concerns and needs to the Father. The Holy Spirit always leads us to do what Jesus is doing. Even as Jesus is praying for us, it is our responsibility to pray for others.

How Meekness Produces Healing

How does meekness produce greater healing and wholeness in us? It removes from us the great burden of self-defense and self-promotion.

How many people do you know who strive to prove themselves to other people? They continually try to build themselves up in order to win approval or praise. They are struggling to raise themselves up to the position where other people will think they are worthy, valuable, lovable, important. Let me assure you, all this striving produces stress. It puts us into ongoing competition with others because in seeking to raise ourselves up, we inevitably find ourselves in a position of putting others down. Those who strive for their own success see every other person in their arena as a rival.

In sharp contrast, the person who yields all glory and honor to God is a person who is freed from a spirit of competition and instead is given a spirit of cooperation. The person who is meek seeks to help others succeed, be helped, be honored.

The meek person desires that others become all that God created them to be. She encourages others to employ their gifts and to use their minds and release their faith. She does not see God's rewards as limited, but rather as *unlimited*—God's rewards are for all people to experience, His success is for all to enjoy, His salvation is for all to accept, His love is for all to receive.

The meekness of the Christian is expressed in terms of appreciation and value for others.

The meek person, in believing that God desires for all people to be transformed from sinners into saints, is a person who knows that the ultimate work of converting lost souls and transforming believers into Christ's nature is *God's work*. We as human beings cannot reproduce godly traits. Only God can reproduce godly characteristics in us. The meek person is freed of all responsibility for transforming others, manipulating others, or controlling others. He knows that his role is to tell others about Jesus, to obey God's commandments, and to manifest godly fruit in all places and to all people. The wooing, winning, saving, healing, transforming work is the work of God. We cannot save another person's soul. Only God can. We cannot heal or restore or deliver another person from evil. Only God can.

When we yield all authority and glory to God, we truly stand in humility before Him. We are yielding *all* to Him, and we stand in position to do His bidding at all times. That, my friend, is meekness.

A person who stands in this position before God and other people experiences far less stress because she knows that God is in charge. Such a person also has far more friends because she is not trying to control or coerce others. Less stress and more friends—that's a combination that always promotes greater emotional, physical, material, and spiritual health. That is the healing work of God's gentle meekness in our lives.

Thirteen

THE HEALING POWER
OF SELF-CONTROL

The Spirit's Control Brings Order to Chaos

In April 1979 something went awry inside a fifty-six-foot nuclear power plant reactor at Three Mile Island. A hydrogen bubble expanded to the size of a room in a typical house. Then suddenly, the bubble shrank to a size smaller than a closet.

The best scientists in America didn't know why the bubble developed, why it expanded, then contracted, or what would happen next. Would it dissipate or would it explode?

A pastor who lived in the area wrote the following:

> Apparently everything is going calmly [now] down at Three Mile Island. I am glad because I live nearby.
>
> My own life is kind of a hydrogen bubble about to blow up, or maybe there is going to be a meltdown. My anxiety about my life is just at an unbearable level. I feel such an awful guilt about things I have done in the past. Like the accident at Three Mile Island, it is due to human error…my errors. Now, just a few sins in my life seem to

have triggered something terrible. I feel as though I will explode, and I need peace. I haven't lost my mind, my children, or my wife. In fact, they really aren't aware of how my life has gotten out of hand.

Can you understand how I feel?

The sad fact is that most people *do* know how this man feels. There's a bubble in them that is expanding and about to explode. And if it does explode, the outcome may be a personal meltdown of some kind—a raging rampage, a heart attack, a spiral into depression. Millions of people are on the brink of being broken in ways that are deep and devastating.

The Old Testament tells us that when a man named Nehemiah heard that the walls of Jerusalem were broken and the gates of the city had been burned, he wept. For days he mourned and fasted and prayed. His heart was broken at the news that Israel's beloved Jerusalem was in ruins.

Broken walls in the ancient Near East were a symbol of total collapse. A city without walls had no defense against those who wanted to pillage and loot. In the eyes of all who saw its ruin, it was a city that had lost its destiny. A city without walls resulted in a people being in "trouble and disgrace," which is how the people of Jerusalem were described to Nehemiah (Nehemiah 1:3).

Many of us can see ourselves in the brokenness of Jerusalem's walls. The Bible tells us, "Like a city whose walls are broken down is a man who lacks self-control" (Proverbs 25:28). A person who leads an undisciplined life is left without any defense against Satan's attacks. A person's lack of self-control will lead to further devastation in every area of his life.

In sharp contrast, our God is a God of order. The forces of nature are kept in balance by His divine hand, as are human politics and all other human enterprises. No nation is beyond His power to control.

Jesus lived in the power of God as He walked the earth. In His humanity, He had to walk along the dusty roads of Galilee and over the cobbled streets of Jerusalem. In His humanity, He had to reach out and touch countless numbers who came to Him for healing or deliverance— sometimes until he reached the point of exhaustion. Jesus didn't walk on air or survive without sleep and food or live in a vacuum isolated from other people. He lived a real life, a disciplined life, a life of choices and decisions. He chose to cooperate fully with God's plan and to discipline His life to accomplish God's goals.

The Holy Spirit calls us to be like Jesus in living a God-ordered life and in remaining totally committed to doing things God's way. The Spirit calls us to maintain a passion for excellence in serving God and others. And the Holy Spirit supplies all the power we need to live a disciplined, God-honoring life.

WHAT IT MEANS TO CONTROL SELF

A pastor from the Midwest once wrote a letter to a Christian magazine in which he bemoaned the influence that television was having on children. He recalled an incident in which he asked his young daughter to memorize the verse that lists the fruit of the Spirit. He said to her, "Come and tell me as soon as you can recite from memory all nine traits that are part of the fruit of the Spirit."

An hour or so later the little girl came to her father and proudly said, "The fruit of the Spirit is love, joy, peace, patience, kindness, goodness, faithfulness, gentleness…and remote control."

We may be confused about self-control, but we are clear on the need for it. People realize their lives are out of control, and they do various things to try to regain the upper hand. They believe that if they work out at the gym regularly, go to church regularly, follow a healthy diet, and refuse to drink, smoke, and use harmful chemical substances, they have their lives "under control."

The sad fact is, however, that most people have no idea what self-control really is. The self-control of the Holy Spirit is not a daily discipline; it is a *character trait.* It is not a list of rules, but a guiding principle that comes from the Spirit indwelling us. It means that we are focused on doing God's will and God's will alone. Self-control is hearing God say, "speak now" and then going ahead to speak, without asking, "But how will people respond?" Self-control is hearing God say, "Go to a certain place, and when you get there do this," and then going to that place and doing what God commands, without making any excuses. That is a practical definition of the self-control that comes through the Holy Spirit.

THE OPPOSITE OF SELF-CONTROL

In an earlier chapter we discussed the widespread misuse of the word *love.* We could say a similar thing about our misunderstanding of self-control. We regularly see people completely missing the meaning of this spiritual fruit in three areas.

It Is Not Self-Mastery

Self-control does not come about through the discipline of self-mastery, but rather through self-surrender. None of us has the power, capability, or wisdom fully to master our own lives. You cannot master the temptations that are hurled at you, the behavior of those closest to you, the feelings that you feel, or the ideas that pop into your mind. You can *respond* to each of these, but you can't control them. None of us is capable of living a fear-free, disease-free, trouble-free life.

Most of the books that promote self-mastery encourage readers to take charge of their lives. These books falsely teach that we can do all things *if we just put our minds to it.* The goal is to control our destiny.

It is amazing that so many fall for this lie. If you look back on all that happened in your life over the past few days, you have to admit that you have no control over the behavior of others—even those you love the most and who love you the most. Parents would love to be able to control the thoughts, words, and deeds of their children. It just isn't possible.

We also must admit that we cannot always control our own selves. We often do what we don't truly want to do. We say no to a temptation one day and find ourselves yielding to it the next. We may be strong in our stance for Christ one day, but waver the next.

Self-mastery is what the Pharisees practiced. They sought to keep not only the Law given to Moses but all of the laws that had been added by the rabbis and scholars through the ages since Moses received the Command-ments of God on Mount Sinai. Jesus, however, could see the thoughts and motives of the Pharisees, and He called what He saw "whitewashed tombs" (Matthew 23:27). He saw deadness. He saw a lack of love and worship of God, and a lack of love and concern for other people.

What each of us does have is an ability to surrender our lives to the Holy Spirit. We can control how we respond, yield, and submit to Him. We can hand over the reins of our lives. As we invite the Holy Spirit to take over the reins of our lives, we experience His power being added to the decisions of our will. This brings genuine *willpower:* His power, and our will, working together under His control.

It Is Not the Loss of All Pleasure

Many people believe self-control requires that we give up anything that brings pleasure. They equate the sinful behaviors of the world with fun, laughter, and good times. They equate the pursuit of the lust of the flesh, the lust of the eyes, and the pride of life with enjoying the best food, the finest parties, the most exciting vacations. To be self-controlled, in contrast, is regarded by these same people as the pursuit of an austere life.

The Stoics who lived in ancient Greece had this grit-your-teeth, deny-life's-pleasures attitude. But this has nothing to do with the Holy Spirit's fruit of self-control. Two problems arise from a person's reliance on *self*-discipline. First, people who live this way often become morbid. They think God calls them to shun happiness. Second, they have little ability to cope with unexpected events. They don't know how to handle a torrent of trouble, but neither do they know how to handle a tidal wave of joy. In the end they miss out on much that is positive and godly!

Self-control is not about shunning things that bring joy. God said about all of His creation, "It is good." He expected man to enjoy the beauty and pleasure of the world He made. He even built celebration into the Israelite way of life with countless feast days—one out of seven days was a day of rest, several weeks a year were holy holidays, several other special feast days were designated for all the people to keep, not to mention the joy of wedding celebrations and parties in honor of babies being born and children coming of age.

God does not call us to morbidity, but to a balance between a genuine enjoyment of His goodness and moderation in consumption of that goodness.

Jesus said:

> John [the Baptist] came neither eating nor drinking, and they say, "He has a demon." The Son of Man came eating and drinking, and they say, "Here is a glutton and a drunkard, a friend of tax collectors and 'sinners.'" But wisdom is proved right by her actions. (Matthew 11:18-19)

Jesus called people to look at the end result of their choices and behavior. For example, does eating to excess make a person happy? Few people would say so, especially after being up much of the night with a stomachache. On the other hand, does eating a fine meal with moderation give us an opportunity to appreciate the variety of foods God has created, the culinary skills of a good cook, and the pleasure of good conversation, laughter, and the warmth of Christian fellowship? Absolutely. We can enjoy such a feast and still be in full submission to the Holy Spirit.

It Is Not Self-Improvement

We are obsessed with the prospect of improving ourselves. Infomercials and magazines promise makeovers that will produce beauty and physical fitness or bring about career advancement and financial reward, and even spiritual overhauls that promise to enhance one's quality of life. The self-improvement gurus tell us we can pull ourselves up by our bootstraps to a higher standard of performance, a higher profile in society, or a higher level of beauty.

There is only one thing wrong with self-improvement: It rarely works.

Human nature is not geared to sticking with disciplined effort that delivers only incremental progress. Instead, we want a pill or a medical procedure that will immediately make us thin, beautiful, wealthy, and happy. We want to fly as fast as we can into a future that we fashion out of our own imagination. And when life doesn't come to us easily and all at once, we get discouraged and give up.

The evidence of this is all around us. Nine out of ten lotto winners are broke within three years. Those who embark on drastic diets nearly always rebound to a greater weight than before the diet. Drug addicts and alcoholics who go off drugs "cold turkey" and make no change in their relationship with God nearly always return to drugs or alcohol.

Another reason self-improvement programs fail is that we set unrealistic goals. We don't just want to have our financial needs met, we want to be rich. We don't just want a good job, we want to reach the top of the corporate ladder by the age of thirty. Rarely do we stop to ask God, "Is this how You want me to live?"

Self-improvement assumes that we can achieve all that we set our minds to. God's Word has a different message: It is God who sets up kings and deposes them (see Daniel 2:21). God brings recognition to certain people in order to further His purposes. So should we never set goals or seek to improve our circumstances in life? My response is this: Ask God what *He* desires for you to have and to work toward.

God's Word says:

> Listen, you who say, "Today or tomorrow we will go to this
> or that city, spend a year there, carry on business and make
> money." Why, you do not even know what will happen
> tomorrow. What is your life? You are a mist that appears for

a little while and then vanishes. Instead, you ought to say,
"If it is the Lord's will, we will live and do this or that."
(James 4:13-15)

God knows what He wants to improve in our lives. If we will yield to
Him, He will fashion us into the likeness of Christ Jesus, provide for all
our needs, and give us the desires of our heart that are in keeping with His
purposes. Self-improvement apart from God's help may work outwardly.
But deep down, the discontent and dissatisfaction remain. In contrast,
God's improvement of us always works perfectly, both inwardly and on
the outside.

Peter wrote:

> His divine power has given us everything we need for life
> and godliness through our knowledge of him who called
> us by his own glory and goodness. Through these he has
> given us his very great and precious promises, so that
> through them you may participate in the divine nature and
> escape the corruption in the world caused by evil desires.
> (2 Peter 1:3-4)

This does not mean that when we ask the Holy Spirit to fill us and
take over the reins of our lives that we can put our spirituality on auto-
pilot. We are always to cooperate with God in the process. He produces
spiritual fruit in us, but we are responsible for manifesting it and making
it available to others.

There once was a boy named Thomas. He was an unpopular boy—
overweight, awkward, and shy. Although his family was rich and quite

influential, Thomas felt isolated. When he reached the age of fourteen, his father sent him to a private school. There, one of his teachers witnessed to him about Christ, and Thomas accepted Jesus as his Savior and Lord.

The other students ridiculed his commitment to Christ. Then one day, for a class assignment, Thomas had to debate the existence of God. In that hour teacher and students alike came to see Thomas as a great thinker. His grasp of logic and his commitment to the truth of the Scriptures brought him respect.

Back home, however, his family was upset. They expected Thomas to return home to take his place in the family business. His older brothers were real playboys, and they were embarrassed that their brother had become a "holy" person. Thomas's brothers decided to kidnap him and hold him prisoner for a year to get him to turn away from God. The "prison" they prepared, however, was the opposite of deprivation. The brothers provided Thomas with everything money could buy, set him up in business, and brought prostitutes to him.

But Thomas didn't yield to any of these enticements. His commitment to Christ and his daily reliance upon the Holy Spirit gave him true biblical self-control. The brothers were bewildered by his refusals of money, power, and sex. Finally, they gave up and let him return to the university.

Thomas continued to love God and pursue what he believed God had called him to be and to do. During his life he wrote eighteen large volumes, including a commentary on nearly every book of the Bible. Thomas Aquinas understood that self-control was not a matter of self-mastery, self-denial, or self-improvement. He understood that biblical self-control was a matter of yielding control of his life to the Holy Spirit, and of asking the Spirit to reveal to him what he needed to be and do in life. When we pursue God's plan for our lives with all our hearts, minds, and wills, that is when we truly are controlled by Him and our lives become disciplined.

THE MYSTERY OF SELF-CONTROL

Here is a great mystery involving the way the Holy Spirit works in us: To be self-disciplined, we must yield control of self. The fact is, we all routinely yield control of our lives to forces outside us. We yield to the law of gravity when we fall. We yield to other motorists in order to avoid automobile accidents. We yield to the wishes of our supervisor at work in order to get a job done.

In writing to the Ephesians, the apostle Paul drew an analogy between a person who loses control of his senses through the use of alcohol and a person who loses control of his life through being filled with the Spirit of God. He said, "Do not get drunk on wine, which leads to debauchery. Instead, be filled with the Spirit. Speak to one another with psalms, hymns and spiritual songs. Sing and make music in your heart to the Lord, always giving thanks to God the Father for everything, in the name of our Lord Jesus Christ" (Ephesians 5:18-20).

If you do not invite the Holy Spirit to fill up your life, the inner you will be filled with the impulses of the world, the flesh, and the devil. None of us walks around as a spiritual void. We all have something working inside us. You *will* be filled, either with God's Spirit or with the decaying influence of the devil, the world, or the lusts of your own flesh.

Jesus made this clear. Some of the people who had seen Him deliver a man from a demonic spirit said about Jesus, "By Beelzebub, the prince of demons, he is driving out demons" (Luke 11:15). Jesus knew what they were thinking, and He responded:

Any kingdom divided against itself will be ruined, and a
house divided against itself will fall. If Satan is divided
against himself, how can his kingdom stand?...

When a strong man, fully armed, guards his own
house, his possessions are safe. But when someone
stronger attacks and overpowers him, he takes away the
armor in which the man trusted and divides up the
spoils....

When an evil spirit comes out of a man, it goes
through arid places seeking rest and does not find it. Then
it says, "I will return to the house I left." When it arrives,
it finds the house swept clean and put in order. Then it
goes and takes seven other spirits more wicked than itself,
and they go in and live there. And the final condition of
that man is worse than the first. (Luke 11:17-18,21-22,
24-26)

In essence Jesus was saying, "Either you will be filled with God or the
devil. It's not enough that you have your soul cleansed and put in order.
You must ensure that your soul *stays* in right relationship with God.
Otherwise, the forces of darkness will move in to fill the void."

THE SINS OF PRIDE AND LUST

Have you ever stopped to consider what your life will be filled with if you
do *not* choose to yield your control daily to the filling of the Holy Spirit?

John wrote, "Everything in the world—the cravings of sinful man,
the lust of his eyes and the boasting of what he has and does—comes not

from the Father but from the world" (1 John 2:16). In the *King James Version,* these three forces that work to our grave detriment are called "the lust of the flesh, and the lust of the eyes, and the pride of life."

Rather than drink in life according to our own lusts and pride, we must drink in God, inviting Him to indwell us *fully.* To yield control, we must feed on God's Word. We must rely on the Holy Spirit's convicting power, sensitive to the ways in which He might prick our conscience about what to choose and how to take action.

When the Bible speaks of putting off the old nature and putting on the new nature, it is challenging us to *exercise* the nature of God. The apostle Paul used the analogy of an athlete training for his chosen sport. We are to run to win the prize. We are to pursue with great diligence, preparation, and effort those things that God says are the marks of mature character.

If you don't know how to control your anger, ask God to show you how. Then *practice* controlling your anger. If you don't know how to get your mind out of the gutter and onto the glory of God, ask Him to show you what you must do. In all likelihood He will ask you to steep your mind in His Word. But He also will ask you to refrain from looking at certain television programs, movies, Web sites, and magazines, and instead, to fill your mind with His truth and music that gives Him praise. When God reveals to you specifically what you are to do, *practice it!*

What has the Lord called you to be? What has He asked you to do? In what arena has He set your witness? To answer these questions with specifics, sit down and create a "here's what I must do" list. But don't undertake a self-improvement project and hope God will honor you when you complete it. Rather, ask God to show you His purpose at the outset. Ask Him to show you what He wants from you. And then go do it with all of your heart, mind, and soul (see Matthew 22:37). The way we show our love for the Lord is to obey all that He directs us to be and to do. We are to pursue His call on our life with all of our energy, our intelligence, our passion.

How Self-Control Heals Us

The spiritual fruit of self-control heals us, in large measure, by bringing order to the chaos of life. When we recognize that God has created us, called us, and equipped us to undertake a specific mission, much of our life comes into focus. We know who we are and what we are to accomplish. We know that the foremost goal God has for us is that we follow Jesus as our Lord. As we seek to do His will and not our own, we are free to take risks, speak boldly, and face life honestly. As we place our trust in God, we know that He will take all things that we do with a sincere heart and turn them into something good within the context of His greater plan and purpose.

There is great freedom in living this way. There is also great comfort and hope!

The person who knows that God is in control can relax and experience the best of life. She can enjoy the satisfaction of giving her best effort to the accomplishment of God-revealed goals. It might seem obvious, but when we yield control to God, He *takes control.* He is more than equal to the challenge of making sense of our lives, healing our brokenness, and putting the pieces of our life into an order that not only makes sense but is beautiful.

A woman once noted the beauty of a large stained-glass window at the front of the church where she worshiped. She said,

I thought about what that window looked like in the work-room of the stained-glass maker. There must have been hundreds of bits and pieces of glass lying around. The artist took those pieces and crafted them against a plan, cut them into shape, and placed them in a particular arrangement to create a beautiful image. Then he sealed the pieces together with hot metal.

"My life is a similar work in progress," the woman continued.

The Lord knows all the pieces of my life. He knows which pieces to cut and how to place the pieces so they will conform to His design. He knows how to weld the pieces together and hang them in place so His light is reflected through them to inspire others. He knows how to make something beautiful and whole out of the fragments of my abilities, desires, dreams, and personality traits. Truly, he is the Artisan; I'm just a pile of broken glass. But as I submit my will to God's plan for me, I'm being fashioned into something glorious.

The Lord alone knows how to put together the broken bits of your life. He alone knows how to make you whole—a delight, a person worthy of His light shining through you.

When we yield our lives to the daily filling of the Holy Spirit, we give Him an opportunity to mold us and heal us. He shows us what needs to be removed from our lives and what we must add. He helps us craft a schedule, a set of goals, a new set of habits, dreams, and plans—all of which combine to produce the person He desires us to become.

God doesn't deal with your life just one bit at a time. He is crafting and fashioning the *whole* of you. He is not working His purpose in you so you will gain the admiration of the world. He's working in you so you can reflect His glory. He's making you into a person with whom He desires to live forever.

In yielding control *to* Him, we become controlled *by* Him. The more we align ourselves with His commands and His plan, the more we lead a focused, disciplined, and purposeful life. And in this lifelong process, we become whole.

The Holy Spirit does not control us with the sole intent of healing us, however. He desires that the focused life we lead bless others. We are controlled by Him so that we might win others to Christ. God always calls us to a purpose that will bless others. Using the metaphor of the stained-glass window, He wants to create a scene of our lives that will cause others to be encouraged, uplifted, and helped so they will respond to God.

As the Holy Spirit heals us, certainly we are blessed. But the greater benefit goes to those who receive our embrace of compassion and words of encouragement rather than gestures of anger or acts of retribution. What the Spirit produces in us, the Spirit also gives *through* us to others. As we manifest the fruit of the Spirit, we extend the blessing to God to those around us. This is true spiritual healing.

THE PRICE OF OUR HEALING

I conclude this book where I began, with healing and wholeness. While most people want to be healed and made whole, not all want to pay the price for healing.

It is one thing to want to get rid of the cancer, and it is a whole other thing to be willing to go through surgery and chemotherapy.

It is one thing to want to avoid a heart attack, and it is a whole other thing to be willing to accept the necessary diet and exercise.

In the same way—when it comes to true spirituality—healing and wholeness will come only when we are willing to yield to God's Spirit. The fruit of the Spirit can only be borne by those who are willing to say with John the Baptist: "He must increase, but I must decrease" (John 3:30, KJV).

If you truly desire healing and wholeness, begin today. Say to the Father, "Father, I am truly willing, and if I am fooling myself in thinking that I am willing, then make me willing to be willing. Empty me of myself and fill me with Your Holy Spirit." And then do the same thing again tomorrow and the next day and the next.

Then, my friend, revel in God's healing and wholeness.

Study Guide

BEARING THE SPIRIT'S FRUIT IN DAILY LIFE

Chapter 1: In Search of a Genuine Spirituality

1. How would you define healing in one sentence?

2. On what is your definition of healing based?

3. What, or whom, do you believe to be the source of all genuine healing and wholeness? Why?

4. As you think about your life, what type of healing do you desire most (emotional, physical, relational, spiritual)?

5. How can God touch your life in such a way that He brings you wholeness? Pray to God right now, asking Him to touch the areas of your life that He desires to restore.

Chapter 2: The Holy Spirit's Healing Work

1. Name five attributes, phrases, or concepts that come to mind when you hear the phrase "the Holy Spirit."

2. If a person who is not a Christian asked you: "What is your relationship to the Holy Spirit?" how would you answer? Would your answer be any different if the person confessed that Jesus is his Savior?

3. If you are a believer in Jesus Christ, think about what the Holy Spirit did to "engineer" your conversion. What did He set in place to bring you to God?

4. In the time since you initially placed your trust in Christ, how has the Holy Spirit brought renewal and healing to your mind, emotions, and spirit?

Chapter 3: Understanding the Spirit's Power

1. If the Holy Spirit indwells every believer in Christ, how is it possible that some Christians are not "filled" with the Spirit?

2. What are the primary issues in your life that prevent you at times from being filled with the Holy Spirit?

3. How do you respond to the concept of the "power of the Holy Spirit"? What is the connection between being filled with the Spirit and experiencing His power at work in your life?

4. Can an individual be spiritually strong apart from the work of the Holy Spirit? Why or why not?

5. In what ways do you need the Holy Spirit in your life? Pray right now, asking the Spirit to reveal to you the things that prevent you from experiencing His filling on a daily basis.

Chapter 4: How God's Spirit Makes Us Whole

1. The Bible talks about the ways believers can hinder the work of the Holy Spirit in their lives. Can you identify a time in your past when you *quenched* the Holy Spirit? What would you do differently if a similar situation arose today?

2. Can you identify a time in your past when you *grieved* the Holy Spirit? What might you do differently if a similar situation arose today?

3. What issues prevent you from abiding in Jesus Christ? Make a list in private of those obstacles in your life.

4. Identify several practical ways in which you can begin to abide more constantly in Him. Make a list of specific things you can do differently and choices you can make that will enable you to abide in Christ more fully.

5. What does it mean to be a fruit-bearing Christian? What can you do to bear more fully the character-likeness of Jesus Christ, which is reflected in the fruit of the Spirit?

Chapter 5: The Healing Power of God's Love

1. In what ways have you experienced God's love? Write down five evidences of God's love. Make it a point to tell someone about them.

2. What is the greatest challenge you face in expressing unconditional love to others?

3. Are there areas in your life that are in need of God's loving forgiveness?

4. Is there a person you need to forgive so you might love him or her more fully?

5. Do you believe other people would identify you as a person who manifests God's love? Do you see yourself as a person who both receives and gives genuine love?

Chapter 6: The Healing Power of God's Joy

1. Do you tend to think of joy as being temporary, a matter of favorable circumstances or positive feelings? If so, how can you begin bearing the fruit of joy that is *independent* of what you face in life?

2.   Can you recall a time when your joy was diminished because
     you continually compared yourself to another person? Do you
     still struggle with comparison? In what ways do you believe
     the Holy Spirit desires to free you from this struggle and give
     you joy?

3.   Can you recall a time when your joy was diminished because you
     felt envy or jealousy? Do you still struggle with those feelings? In
     what ways do you believe the Holy Spirit desires to free you from
     these feelings and give you genuine joy?

4.   Would others identify you as a person who reflects genuine joy? Do
     you see yourself as a joyful person? Why or why not?

5.   Recall a time when you truly experienced the joy of the Lord. Stop
     and thank God for the spiritual fruit of joy, and ask Him to help
     you manifest this fruit on a daily basis.

Chapter 7: The Healing Power of God's Peace

1.   If your heart is troubled right now, think about what is stealing your
     peace. What do you believe the Holy Spirit wants to do to give you
     God's peace?

2.   Are you struggling with fear? If so, have you identified the cause of
     that fear? What do you believe the Holy Spirit desires to do to set
     you free from fear?

3.   Are you an anxious person? Can you isolate the reason for your
     anxiety? What do you believe the Holy Spirit desires to do to over-
     whelm your anxiety with God's peace?

4.   Do you believe other people would identify you as a person who
     experiences and displays God's peace? Do you see yourself as a per-
     son filled with genuine peace? Why or why not?

5. In what ways has God given you His peace? Thank Him for the spiritual fruit of peace, and ask Him to help you manifest this fruit on a daily basis.

Chapter 8: The Healing Power of God's Patience

1. Are you angry with someone? If so, is this a passing emotion or a nagging anger that simmers below the surface? What are you doing about that emotion?

2. How do you believe the Holy Spirit desires to help you respond to those who reject, hurt, or criticize you?

3. If you struggle with impatience, can you identify what most often triggers these behaviors? What do you believe the Holy Spirit wants to do to produce His patience in you?

4. Do you believe other people would identify you as a person who manifests God's patience? Do you see yourself as a patient person? Why or why not?

5. In what ways has God extended His patience to you? Stop and thank God for the spiritual fruit of patience, and ask Him to help you manifest this fruit on a daily basis.

Chapter 9: The Healing Power of God's Kindness

1. Do you struggle with being kind to yourself? If so, how does the Holy Spirit desire to help you in this struggle?

2. Do you find it difficult to receive acts of kindness from others? How do you believe the Holy Spirit wants you to respond to others who seek to show you kindness?

3. Are you harboring hatred toward another person? In what ways do you believe the Holy Spirit desires to heal this hatred?

4. Do you believe other people perceive you to be a genuinely kind person? Do you see yourself as a kind person? Why or why not?

5. In what ways has God shown His kindness to you? Stop and thank God for the spiritual fruit of kindness, and ask Him to help you manifest this fruit on a daily basis.

Chapter 10: The Healing Power of God's Goodness

1. We know the goodness of God through knowing the truth about God. Can you identify times in the past when you have believed lies? What did it mean to you to finally learn the truth?

2. Is there an area in your life in which you seem to be repeatedly deceived? How can you grow in God's truth and resist the deception of Satan?

3. Do you struggle to think good thoughts, to say good words, or to express good emotions? If so, in what ways do you believe the Holy Spirit wants to help you in this struggle?

4. Have you had an experience in doing good to someone who was persecuting you? What was the outcome?

5. In what ways have you been the recipient of God's goodness? Thank God for the spiritual fruit of goodness, and ask Him to help you manifest this fruit on a daily basis.

Chapter 11: The Healing Power of God's Faithfulness

1. Can others count on you to follow through on your commitments and to tell the truth even when it puts you in a bad light? If not, why is this the case?

2. Has anyone found it hard to trust you or to believe things you have told them? If so, what caused this person to question your integrity?

3. Have you ever diminished your relationship with God by pushing it to the margins of your life? If so, what was the outcome?

4. In what ways do you struggle with faithfulness? In what ways do you believe the Holy Spirit desires to help you in that struggle?

5. How have you experienced God's faithfulness in your life? Thank God for the spiritual fruit of faithfulness, and ask Him to help you manifest this fruit consistently in your life.

Chapter 12: The Healing Power of God's Gentleness

1. Have you ever thought of meekness (gentleness) as being weakness? Have you ever considered meek people to be wishy-washy? In what ways do you feel challenged to change your understanding of the word *meek*?

2. Do you know a person who is a "gentle giant"? What character traits or behaviors does that person manifest?

3. Do you ever struggle with trying to prove yourself? What is usually the result? In what ways do you believe the Holy Spirit wants to help you in that struggle?

4. Do other people perceive you to be a person who expresses God's gentleness by bearing the spiritual fruit of meekness? If not, what prevents you from bearing this spiritual fruit?

5. In what ways have you experienced God's gentleness? Thank God for the spiritual fruit of gentleness and meekness, and ask Him to help you manifest this fruit on a daily basis.

Chapter 13: The Healing Power of Self-Control

1. The spiritual fruit of self-control is actually the choice to submit control of our lives to the Holy Spirit. In that light, what does the phrase "submit your life to God" mean to you?

2. One definition of *willpower* is the exercise of the human *will* in concert with the *power* of the Holy Spirit. Can you think of a time when your obedience to the Spirit's leading resulted in the manifestation of His power in your life?

3. Have you completely surrendered your life to God? Are there areas of your life you seek to control by your own ability, intelligence, or self-discipline? What can you do to hand over control of these areas to the Holy Spirit?

4. Do others think of you as a person who is under God's control? Why or why not? How do you see yourself in this regard?

5. In what ways have you experienced the willpower that comes from your will submitted to the power of the Holy Spirit? Thank God right now for the spiritual fruit of self-control, and ask Him to help you manifest this fruit on a daily basis.

Conclusion: The Price of Our Healing

1. What are you ready to sacrifice in order to follow God's Holy Spirit into healing and wholeness?

2. Which areas of your life most need the healing work of the Holy Spirit? Stop and pray about those needs.

3. Do you need to pray this prayer: "Father, empty me of myself and fill me with Your Holy Spirit"? If so, spend time today and in the next few days praying this prayer of faith.

4. In what ways do you perceive the presence of the Holy Spirit in
    your life as He makes you whole? In what ways do you believe He
    is healing you? In what ways is He calling you to be an agent of
    His healing in the lives of others?

Notes

Chapter 1

1. John Naisbitt and Patricia Aburdene, *Megatrends 2000: Ten New Directions for the 1990's* (New York: William Morrow and Co., 1990), 293.

2. Christopher Blake, "New Age, Old Myths," *Message* (November 1989): 6-7.

3. John Dart, "New Age Ideas and Theological Vacuum: Can Churches Resist the Pull of Paranormal?" *The Los Angeles Times* (14 February 1987): 114-5.

4. Alan Bunce, "Searching for Secrets in the Stars," *Christian Science Monitor* (5-6 July 1988): 1-2.

5. Dave Bass, "Drawing Down the Moon," *Christianity Today* (29 April 1991): 14-9.

6. Mike Oppenheimer, "The New Age Movement," *Forbes* (June 1987).

Chapter 2

1. John Calvin, *Institutes of the Christian Religion,* bk. 3, chap. 7, trans. Henry Beveridge. Found at www.reformed.org/books/institutes/bk3ch07.html.

Chapter 5

1. Oscar Wilde, "Phrases and Philosophies for the Use of the Young," *The Chameleon* (December 1894).

2. Robert H. Schuller, *Self Love* (New York: Jove Publications, 1997), 32.

3. Gary Wills, "Robertson and the Reagan Gap," *Time* (22 February 1988).

Chapter 6

1.   C. S. Lewis, *Reflections on the Psalms* (San Diego, Calif.: Harvest Books, 1964).

Chapter 7

1.   Robert Samuelson, "A Few Minutes of Your Time Oppressed by the Scarcity of Time…" *Chicago Tribune* (6 June 1997): 23.

Chapter 8

1.   Marcia K. Hornok, "Psalm 23—Antithesis." Used by permission.

Chapter 9

1.   John S. Tompkins, "Our Kindest City," *Reader's Digest* (July 1994): 55.

Chapter 11

1.   George MacDonald (1824–1905), *The Marquis of Lossie* (n.p.: Johannesen, reprint ed. 1995).

2.   Steve Farrar, *Finishing Strong* (Sisters, Oreg.: Multnomah, 2000).

3.   P. G. Mathew, M.A., M.Div., Th.M., "Chariots of Fire, Part Two," Grace Valley Christian Center. From October 1, 2000 sermon transcript. Found at www.dcn.davis.ca.us/~gvcc/sermon_trans/2000/Chariots_of_Fire_2.html.

Chapter 12

1.   Henry G. Bosh, "The Reward of Humility," *Our Daily Bread* (Grand Rapids: RBC Ministries, 4 August 1973). Used by permission.

2.   Leonard Ravenhill, "Strings for Your Harp, Part III. The Church., D. The Lukewarm Church," *Heart Breathings* (Hampton, Tenn.: Harvey Christian Publishers, L.L.P., 1995). Found at www.ravenhill.org/heartb17.htm. Used by permission.